MATHEMATICAL INVESTIGATIONS

BOOK TWO

A Series of Situational Lessons

Networks • Sports Math

Discovering Rules

Exploring Rates • Using Maps

Randall Souviney

Murray Britt

Salvi Gargiulo

Peter Hughes

DALE SEYMOUR PUBLICATIONS

This book is printed on recycled paper.

This U.S. edition is adapted from *Investigations in Mathematics* by
M. Britt, S.V. Gargiulo, and P. Hughes (Auckland, New Zealand:
New House Publishers, 1988).

The "Chart of General Equations" (page 49) originally appeared in *Finite Differences* by D. Seymour
and M. Shedd (Palo Alto, CA: Dale Seymour Publications, 1973). Used by permission of the publisher.

Cover design: Rachel Gage
Illustrations: Edith Allgood (for Dale Seymour Publications); Felicity Blake
and Warren Mahy (for New House Publishers)

Order number DS21101
ISBN 0-86651-541-0

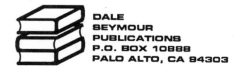

DALE
SEYMOUR
PUBLICATIONS
P.O. BOX 10888
PALO ALTO, CA 94303

4 5 6 7 8 9 10-MA-96 95

CONTENTS

PREFACE

Solving a problem often requires looking at a situation from a different point of view. For example, imagine you are sitting in a room looking through a 10-foot-tall rectangular window. Suddenly a wheel with a 100-mile radius rolls past at 100 miles per hour. What would you see? Would the wheel quickly block out the light to the window? How would the edge of the wheel appear as it passed the window? If you were not initially aware of what it was, could you predict the shape of the object as it passed?

One way to start thinking about this problem is to remember times when trains or other objects have moved past you quickly. The window might suddenly get dark as the wheel arrived, stay dark for a while, then, just as suddenly, get light again as the wheel departed. This explanation agrees with common experience and seems like a reasonable prediction. However, in this case past experience is misleading. When objects are very large (or very small), common experience may not provide useful models.

To explain what actually happens, mentally move away from the window and wheel (perhaps 50 miles or so) to see them both in perspective. From this point of view, the window is very small compared to the wheel. In fact, much of the wheel will pass by the window without your even being aware of it. When the contact point between the wheel and the ground gets close enough to the window, the edge of the wheel comes into view at the top of the window. Since the wheel is so large, the edge appears almost parallel to the ground and will gradually cover the window from top to bottom like a shade being pulled. As the wheel passes the window, the edge moves in the opposite direction like a shade being raised. It would be nearly impossible for you—or any observer inside the room—to tell the difference between a huge wheel passing a window and a shade being slowly pulled and raised.

How long does it take the edge of the wheel to complete one shade-pulling-and-raising cycle? There are a number of ways to investigate this problem mathematically. One approach, using algebra, is presented step-by-step below. This is just one example of how a student—or teacher—might conduct a mathematical investigation of such an intriguing problem.

To determine how long one shade-pulling-and-raising cycle takes, make a drawing:

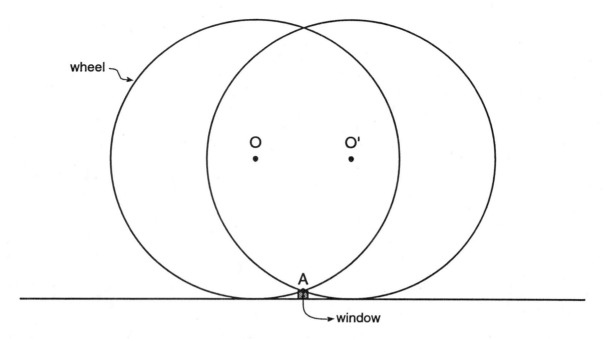

wheel —↗

O   O'

A

↳ → window

The drawing indicates the position of the wheel when it's first visible from the window (the left circle) and when the wheel is almost past (the right circle). This represents one shade-pulling-and-raising cycle. Point *A* is where the two circles intersect.

Next, draw in the radius of the wheel and construct a triangle. Consider △OO', where OA = O'A = the radius of the wheel—and OO' is the distance the center of the wheel moves in one shade-pulling-and-raising cycle.

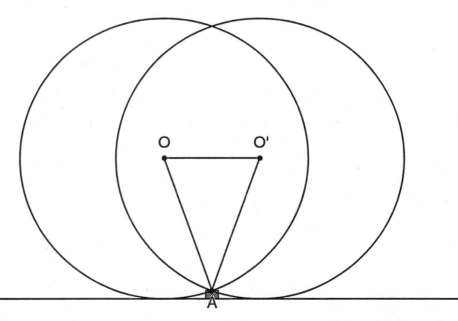

O   O'

A

Since Distance (*d*) = Rate (*r*) × Time (*t*), the amount of time it takes the wheel to complete one cycle can be found by

$$t = \frac{d}{r}$$

where *d* = OO' and *r* = the speed of the wheel.

Use the Pythagorean Theorem and a scientific calculator to find the distance the wheel moves in one shade-pulling-and-raising cycle (OO'). Remember: Since the radius is 100 miles and the window 10 feet, you must convert miles to feet.

$$a^2 + b^2 = c^2$$
$$b = \text{radius} - 10 \text{ feet}$$
$$\text{radius } (c) = 100 \text{ miles } (528{,}000 \text{ feet})$$
$$a^2 + (527{,}990)^2 = (528{,}000)^2$$
$$a = 3{,}249.6 \text{ feet}$$
$$\text{So } OO' = 2a = 6{,}499.2 \text{ feet.}$$

Now solve for t (Time):

$$t = \frac{6{,}499.2 \text{ feet}}{100 \text{ mph}} = \frac{6{,}499.2 \text{ feet}}{528{,}000 \text{ feet ph}}$$

$t = 0.0123$ hours $= 0.74$ minute (or about 45 seconds).

So, it takes about one minute (0.74) to complete one shade-pulling-and-raising cycle when the wheel has a radius of 100 miles and is traveling 100 miles per hour. What would happen if the wheel had a 1,000-mile radius, or was traveling at 50, 200, 400, or 800 miles per hour? Investigating this problem should generate many interesting number patterns.

As this example illustrates, sometimes we can better understand the phenomena we see in nature and society by using mathematical tools and reasoning. *Mathematical Investigations* is a series of three books for the secondary school level, designed to develop students' mathematical reasoning abilities in everyday situational lessons. In this Book Two of the series, the investigations are grouped into five chapters, introducing fundamental mathematical ideas in the context of networks, sports math, finite-difference patterns (rules), rates, and using maps. These topics were selected not only because they appeal to the interests of secondary students, but also because each provides unique opportunities to develop a specific approach to mathematical problem solving.

Each investigation involves one or more applications of algebra, geometry, graphing, counting, probability, and statistics in solving practical problems; at the same time, it teaches a kind of reasoning that cuts across all grade levels and many mathematical fields. By examining certain aspects of real-world situations while working on their own through a guided discovery process, students can develop confidence in using mathematics in their everyday lives, whether or not they intend to pursue a mathematics-based career.

These materials support a number of the recommendations made in the *Curriculum and Evaluation Standards for School Mathematics,* published in 1989 by the National Council of Teachers of Mathematics (NCTM), as well as the principles stated in state curriculum overviews such as California's *Mathematics Framework.* These documents recommend that mathematics be presented *not* as a collection of concepts and skills to be mastered but rather as a variety of methods for investigating and thinking about problems. In this type of curriculum, the students, rather than being passive absorbers of information, become more self-directed, taking an active role as they make conjectures, discover and abstract relationships from problem situations, verify assertions, reason and explain their reasoning, and generally construct their own meaning.

This book, then, bears little resemblance to a traditional mathematics textbook; neither is it one of the familiar collections of discrete supplementary activities that teachers can dole out for practice, extension, or review. Instead, this is a book of challenging, interconnected situational lessons linked together in the sequences that we call *investigations.* Teaching notes at the beginning of each chapter explain the important mathematical and scientific generalizations to be presented. The investigations follow, each consisting of a series of questions, exercises, and increasingly more complex problems carefully sequenced to help students identify a solution strategy, which in turn leads them to important generalizations. Many of the questions require essay-type answers:

> *Explain her reasoning.*
>
> *Explain why this would be true.*
>
> *Why is this a losing strategy?*
>
> *Explain how the diagram works.*

Students may not be accustomed to writing long verbal answers for their math exercises, but expressing new concepts in their own words is a proven way to help them clarify their reasoning.

While the pages of this book are reproducible, they *cannot* be regarded as single-page handouts; each investigation, ranging from 4 to 14 pages, must be duplicated as a complete packet so that students can work through it from beginning to end. Within a given investigation, students will encounter special extension activities called "On Your Own" that generally involve independent experimentation or research, some of which may have to take place outside of class.

Throughout the investigations, students will learn to use such general problem-solving tools as *trying simpler cases, conducting experiments, looking for patterns, using the guess-and-check tactic, looking for symmetry, and using logical reasoning.* They also use more specific tools such as *constructing tables, making models, graphing data, drawing sketches, making systematic lists,* and *writing formulas* as they work to unravel the underlying relationships in a problem. Teachers should remind and encourage students to try one or more of these tools as they investigate each new problem situation. Additionally, it is assumed that students will have access to hand-held calculators at all times and will use them freely in the computation involved in these investigations.

A "Check-up" quiz at the end of each chapter gives students a chance to check their understanding of the principles and procedures that they encountered in the investigations.

Because the concepts underlying these investigations are drawn from more than one area of mathematics, we have included in each book a collection of 35 KeyMath concepts that students may need to review. As students work through the investigations, they will periodically see in the margin a small key symbol with a number inside, referring them to a particular KeyMath concept. Teachers may want to have several sets of the KeyMath section duplicated and available for student reference. Students who need help can turn to this section to find a brief discussion of the concept followed by a short set of practice exercises.

Answers for exercises and problems in both the investigations and the KeyMath section are included at the end of the book.

CHAPTER ONE

Networks

TEACHING NOTES

Networks are a collection of points (vertices) on a surface interconnected with lines (edges) that encompass one or more regions. A map of cities connected with roads can be thought of as a network. The study of network *graphs* was originally proposed by Léonard Euler in 1736 in a paper on the impossibility of traversing the seven bridges of Königsberg. Note that a network is *connected* if all the vertices are joined by a continuous path—in other words, the network is in one piece.

Investigation One • The Mailcarrier Problem

The Mailcarrier Problem involves evaluating a network of roads (edges) and road intersections (vertices) to determine if a route can be designed that allows the mailcarrier to visit each mailbox without the inefficiency of retracing steps. The solution depends on the number of odd and even vertices contained within a network. An *odd* vertex has an odd number of roads connecting it to other vertices, and an *even* vertex has an even number of connecting roads. Euler discovered that a network can be *traversed*—that is, the mailcarrier can visit all the mailboxes without using the same road twice— only if there are exactly *zero* or *two* odd vertices. If all the vertices are even (there are zero odd vertices), the mailcarrier can start at any vertex and find a path that can be traversed. However, if there are two odd vertices (and any number of even vertices), the mailcarrier needs to plan a path that starts at one of the odd vertices and ends at the other. This does not solve the Mailcarrier Problem, since the mailcarrier may have to start at any point in the network and may not end up at the starting position. To solve the problem, some part of the network must be retraced. If there are four, six, eight, or more odd vertices (there only can be an even number of odd vertices), further retracing is required to solve the problem. Students do experiments and organize the results in tables to find the odd/even vertices pattern.

Investigation Two • Shortest Routes

Determining the minimal distance and time to traverse from point A to point B in a network can be accomplished using a *tree diagram*. A tree diagram is a systematic way to ensure that all possible routes and time combinations are considered when calculating optimal distances and times. Students are asked to use tree diagrams to determine the shortest distance between locations on a map and the best routes when travel conditions and stoplights affect commuting time.

Investigation Three • Connected Networks

Connecting points to form *connected networks* are explored in this investigation. Students are asked to evaluate the efficiency of plans to connect water sprinklers with pipe and towns with telephone cables. By looking for a pattern in a series of investigations, students develop the formula $n = p - 1$, which relates the number of points p and the minimum number of edges n necessary to connect the points.

Investigation One

The Mailcarrier Problem

A *network* is a collection of points connected by lines that surround one or more regions. Think of the roads (lines) and road intersections (points) a mailcarrier travels to make deliveries as a network.

1 A rural mailcarrier lives in town A. He delivers mail along each road. Can he start from town A, deliver the mail, and return to his home without going along any road twice?

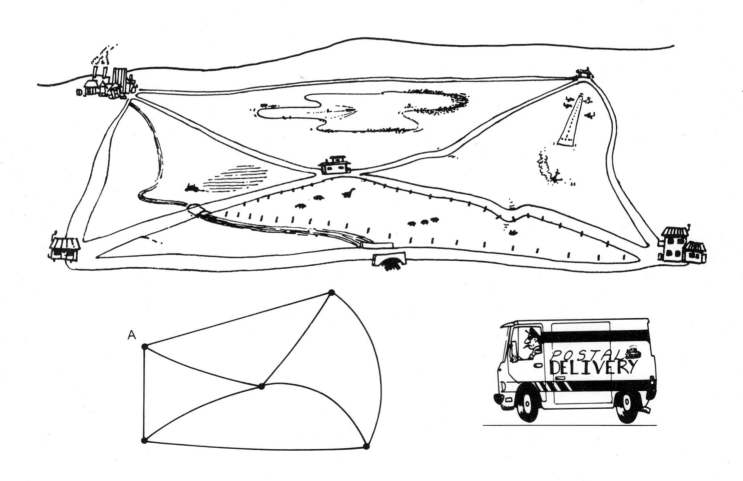

2 Another mailcarrier lives in town B. Does the Mailcarrier Problem have a solution for the region she travels?

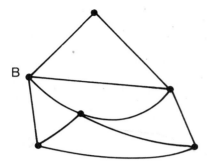

3 The post office employs a mathematician to solve the Mailcarrier Problem. She wisely decides to look at some simple *networks* to see if she can find some rules. She calls the points *vertices* and labels them odd (O) and even (E).

The mailcarrier lives at X in each case.

a Why are some vertices *odd* and others *even*?

b Investigate which of the following networks have solutions to the Mailcarrier Problem. Note that a dead end is a vertex but may create problems for the mailcarrier.

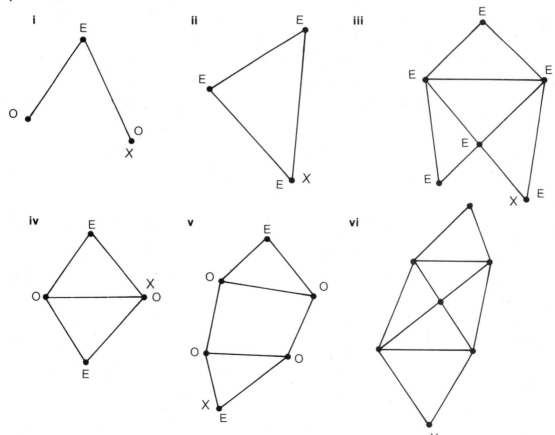

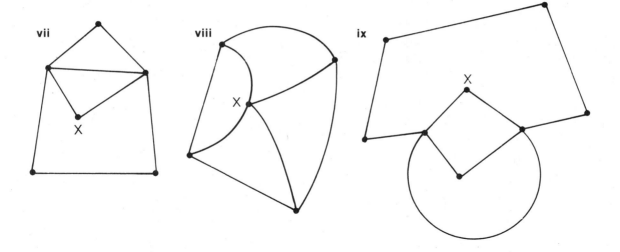

c   Use your answers to **b** to copy and complete this table.

Network	Number of Odds	Number of Evens	Is There a Solution?
i	2	1	No
ii	0	3	Yes
iii			
iv			
v	4		No
vi			
vii			
viii			
ix	0		

d   From the pattern in the table in **c**, the mathematician sees a simple
rule to solve the Mailcarrier Problem. What is her rule? Make up
some of your own networks to confirm the rule.

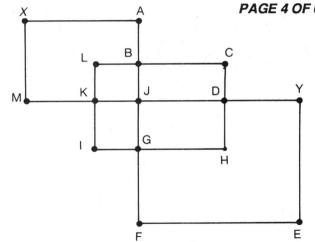

4 a Lisa, a mailcarrier, is stationed at the post office marked X. Show one possible path that Lisa can take to travel along all the roads in the network only once.

b If Lisa was transferred to the post office at Y, does the Mailcarrier Problem still have a solution?

c Investigate whether there is any place on the network where a post office could be in which there is no solution to the Mailcarrier Problem.

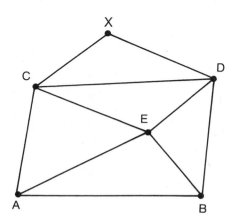

5 For this network, the Mailcarrier Problem starting at post office X can't be solved. However, by going along one particular road twice the problem *can* be solved. Find out which road this is. Is there any place on the network where the post office could be moved that would allow a solution to the Mailcarrier Problem?

On YOUR OWN

Find out the routes used by your mailcarrier to deliver mail. Investigate whether or not this route is the best (the quickest).

6 If a post office is at X, the Mailcarrier Problem cannot be solved for this network. So the mailcarrier redraws the network by adding an extra imaginary road connecting A and B.

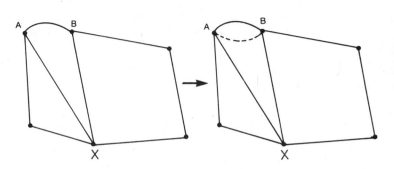

a Can the Mailcarrier Problem be solved in the new network?

b How would the mailcarrier solve the problem starting at X?

7 Solve the Mailcarrier Problem for these networks. Start at X in each case. Clearly mark where roads should be added to allow the mailcarrier to deliver all mail without retracing any steps.

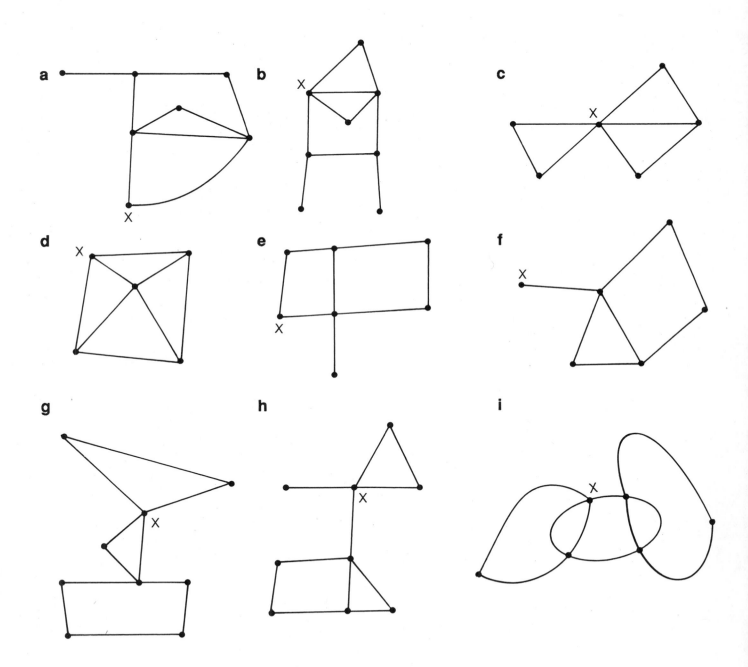

ON YOUR OWN

Find a park or school that has concrete pathways. Also look for any well-used routes that are *not* the concrete pathways. Do these added routes make it easier to move around the site without retracing any paths? Can you suggest ways in which landscape architects might plan where to put pathways in public parks?

Investigation Two

Shortest Routes

1 Henry wants to drive from Geralville to Menzies in the least amount of time. (The travel time between cities is indicated on the map.)

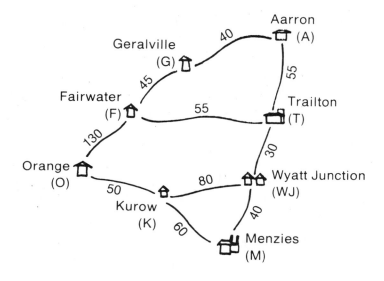

a Complete the tree diagram.
(Times in minutes are shown.)

b What is the minimum travel time?

c What is the answer in **b** if Henry must visit his mother and father in Kurow on the way to Menzies?

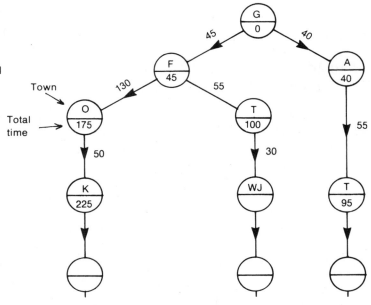

2 a Prepare a tree diagram that shows all reasonable routes between A and E.

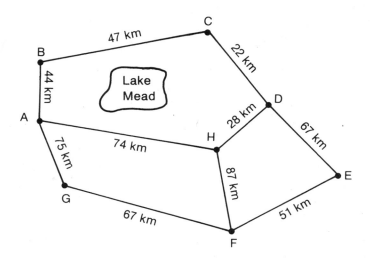

b What is the shortest route between A and E?

3 a Prepare a tree diagram to show all reasonable routes between A and G.

b Which route is the best?

c If a traveler must go through E, which route is best?

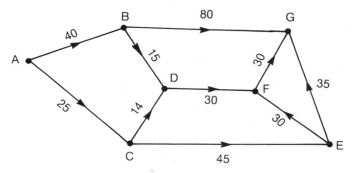

4 A motorist wants to go from A to H through this one-way road system.

a Find her shortest route.

b If she has to stop at E, what would be her best route?

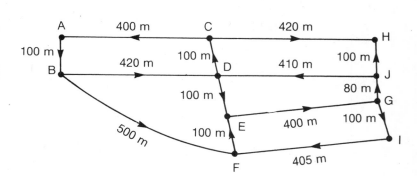

5 This map shows the distances between towns and the average safe driving speeds.

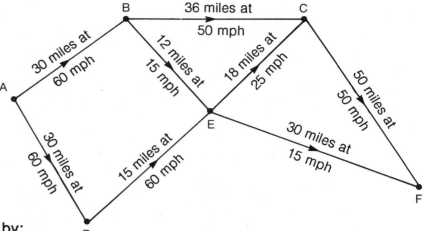

Find the best route from A to F by:

a cutting down the distance traveled.

b cutting down the travel time.

6 Idealtown is planned on a square grid. Park areas are shaded and not crossed by roads. Mickie wants to find the shortest route from A to B. She starts numbering the squares as shown here.

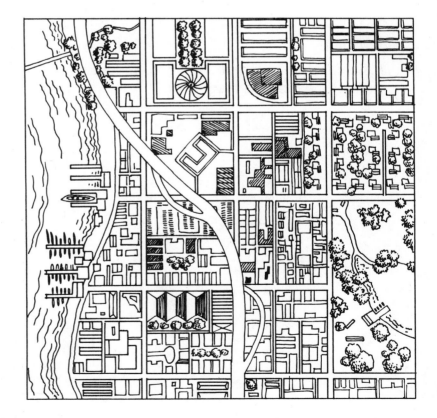

a Complete Mickie's diagram.

b Show the shortest routes on your diagram.

---

7 Squaretown is designed like Idealtown in **6.**

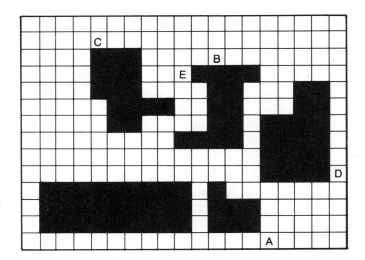

Make four copies of Squaretown on square graph paper. On these, show the shortest routes from:

a A to B.

b A to C.

c C to D.

d D to E.

8 Josie can commute from home to work using a number of different routes. She draws a rough map.

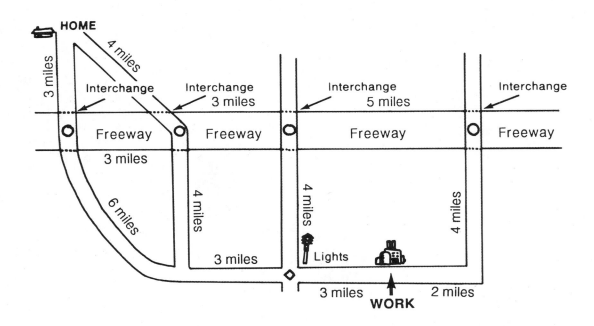

In light traffic, Josie takes one unit of time to travel one mile on the freeway, but she takes two units of time to go one mile on ordinary surface streets. Getting through a traffic light takes two units of time on the average. Now Josie prepares a best-time map. One possible route is marked in time units below.

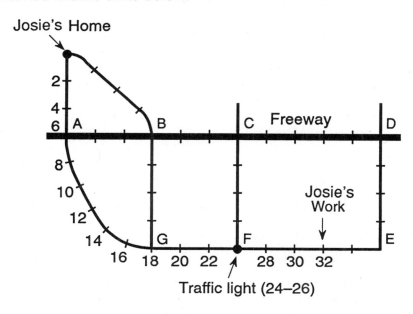

a Complete her time map to determine the way Josie should go to work. Hint: Mark the time units for the different routes.

	Time (units)		
	Morning	**Lunchtime**	**Evening**
Freeway (per mile)	1.0	1.2	2.5
Surface Street (per mile)	2.5	1.8	2.0
Traffic Light (average)	3.0	2.2	3.0

b From the table, prepare three best-time maps to work out Josie's best route:

i in the morning.

ii at lunchtime.

iii in the evening.

Investigation Three

Connected Networks

1 As part of an environmental project, a landscaper plans to place sprinklers at A, B, C, D, and E in a park. M is the point of connection to the water main.

Jan, the accountant for the project, realizes that a number of pipes are unnecessary and just add to the cost.

a She removes pipe BE from the plan. Explain her reasoning.

b The longest pipe left is AB, but she cannot remove it. Why not?

c The next longest pipe is DE. Can she remove it?

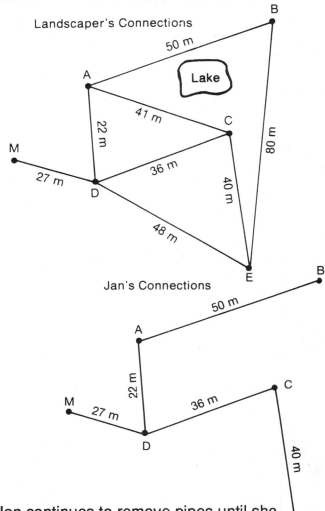

Landscaper's Connections

Jan's Connections

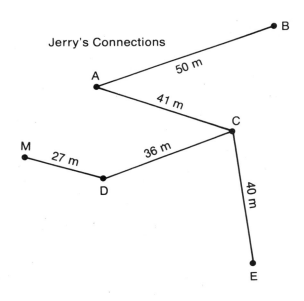

Jerry's Connections

d Jan continues to remove pipes until she reaches the *connected network* shown. Copy the original landscaper's connections and follow Jan's method to get her connections.

e Jerry, Jan's assistant, suggests an alternative. Will Jerry's connected network get water to all sprinklers?

f Show that Jan's connections are shorter (and therefore cheaper) overall.

g i Make a number of networks like Jan's and Jerry's.

ii Confirm that Jan's connected network has the minimum length.

2 Find the shortest (and therefore cheapest) network to connect towns A, B, C, D, E, and F together by telephone. Cables must follow the roads. Make a copy of the original network first.

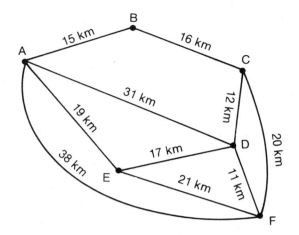

3 In each of the following, find the shortest network that connects all points and write down this length. Make a copy of each original network first.

A.

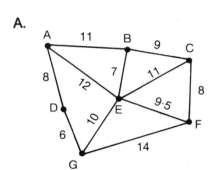

B.

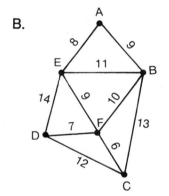

C.

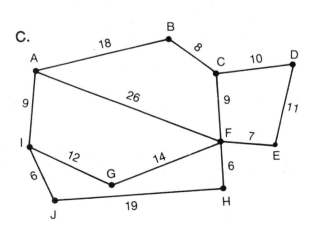

D.

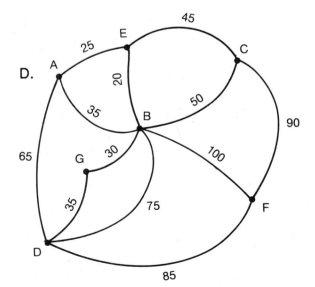

4 Tony suspects there is a simple rule to predict the minimum number of line segments needed for a connected network. He marks four points and draws segments in various ways so there are no unnecessary line segments when the network is connected. Here are two examples.

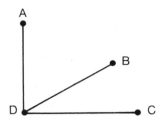

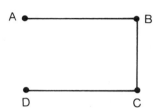

a i Find all the ways of drawing a connected network with the four points and no unnecessary line segments.

ii Do all your answers in **a i** require exactly three line segments?

b Draw connected networks without any unnecessary line segments using:

i two points.

ii three points.

iii five points.

(Note the number of line segments required in each case.)

c Let p = number of points and n = number of line segments to make a connected network without unnecessary segments.

Complete the table.

p	n
2	
3	
4	3
5	
20	
81	

$$n = p - \square$$

d i Explain why a network based on six points that has six line segments must contain an unnecessary line segment.

ii Confirm the statement in **d i** by drawing some examples.

e i Explain why a network based on seven points that has five line segments must be disconnected.

ii Confirm the statement in **e i** by drawing some examples.

5 Explain how the results in **4** can be used to help check your answers for shortest connected-network problems.

ON YOUR OWN

Make your own networks.

See if you can find an example where Jan's rules do *not* give a connected network of the shortest length.

6 Find the connected networks of shortest length for this network. (There is more than one answer.)

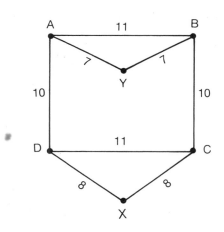

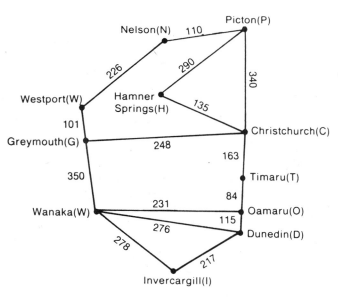

7 Reliable Phones, Inc. wishes to establish a network among the towns shown. Telephone cable costs $5,000 per kilometer to lay. Find the minimum cost of such a network.

8 Note the distances between these towns in Maine. Then find the shortest connected network.

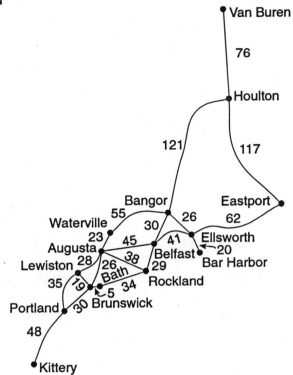

ON YOUR OWN

Make a copy of the map. Design the shortest network connecting all the towns.

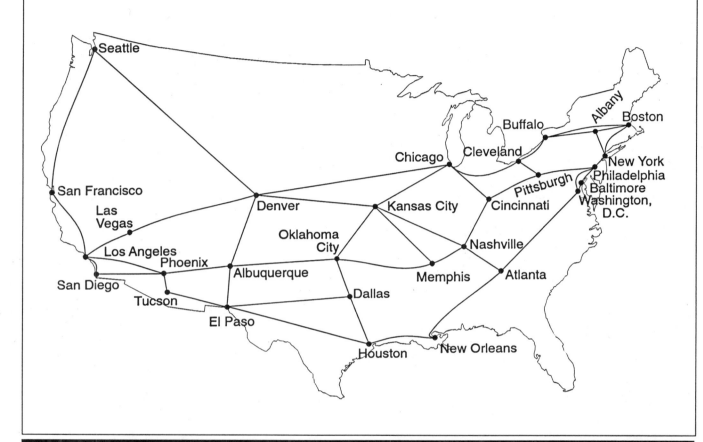

9   An engineer designs a phone system to connect towns A, B, C, D, E, and F. All costs for laying cable are $1,000 per mile, except for cables CE, DE, and FE. Town E is in mountainous country, so costs are $2,000 per mile for cables laid to E.

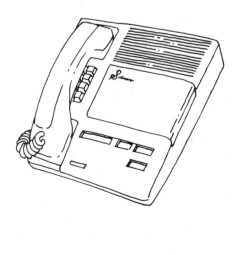

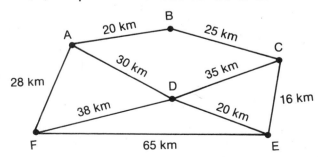

a   Complete the *cost* network.

b   i   Design a smallest *cost* connected network.

ii   What is the cost of your connected network?

Cost network

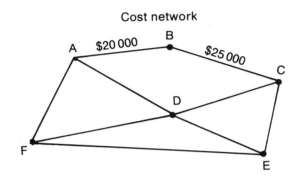

10 Design the smallest cost network for connecting A, B, C, D, and E with phone cables.

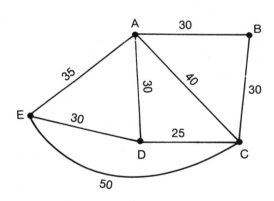

Costs per mile of cable
($ thousands)

A	B	C	D	E	
	5	7	6	7	**A**
		8	X	X	**B**
			10	8	**C**
				9	**D**
					E

CHECK-UP

For each network:

a Find the shortest route from X to Y.

b Solve the Mailcarrier Problem. (The mailcarrier starts and ends at X in each case.)

c Find the shortest connected network.

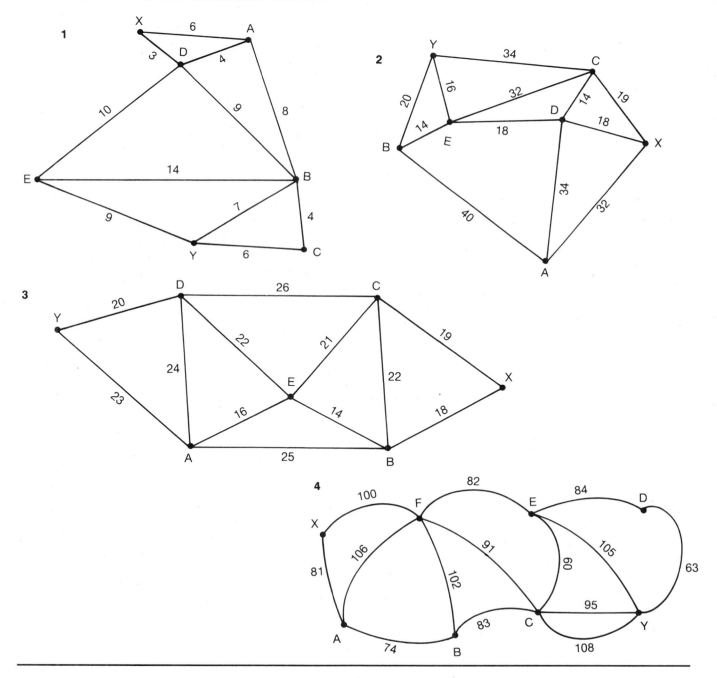

CHAPTER TWO

SPORTSMATH

TEACHING NOTES

The world of sports, always of interest to students, provides a number of interesting mathematical investigations. In this chapter, students apply mathematics in the use of symmetry, systematic lists, and rates to solve sports-related problems.

Investigation One • Tournaments

In this investigation, students are introduced to the special terminology of tournament organizers. Assigning teams in a tournament using a *round-robin* schedule, in which each team plays every other team only once, is called the tournament *draw*. The games are played in *rounds*, since a team can only play one opponent at a time. Students explore the symmetric form of a round-robin table and extend the draw to *n* teams. If there is an even number of teams, all the teams pair off and play simultaneously. For an odd number of teams, one team must be assigned a *bye* and will not play that round. In either case, there will be $\frac{n(n-1)}{2}$ games played if there are *n* teams in the tournament.

Investigation Two • Systematic Counting

The scoring of several sports is explored through use of systematic lists. Each game has a unique scoring scheme that allows only certain total scores. For example, in professional football, a team can score the following points: point-after—1; safety—2; field goal—3; touchdown—6. A football team with a final score of 8 could have scored: 1 touchdown and 1 safety; 2 field goals and 1 safety; or 4 safeties. Students explore the scoring of other games, including basketball, sharpshooting, and soccer. The importance of listing all possible combinations of scores in a systematic pattern ensures that no options are left out.

Investigation Three • Using Rates

The average speed of racers determines who will win. First students explore the fallacy of trying to determine the average speed of a race by calculating the mean speed of all the laps. For example, if you ran one 400-meter lap at 10 meters per second and the second lap at 2 meters per second, the average speed is *not* 6 meters per second $\frac{10+2}{2}$ but 3.3 meters per second.

It would take 40 seconds to run the first lap and 200 seconds to run the second, so $\frac{800 \text{ meters}}{240 \text{ seconds}} \approx 3.3$ meters per second. (That is, you spend much more time at the slower speed, so the faster lap does not compensate as much as first imagined.)

Another application of rates is batting averages. A softball player's batting average is the rate of successful hits compared to the total number of times the player is at a bat. A player who has 25 hits out of 100 times at bat has a batting average of 0.250. This number is often read as a batting average of 250, but it really means 250 thousandths. (Note: In professional baseball, walks and sacrifice flies are *not* counted as times at bat.)

Batting averages themselves can't be averaged, since they are represented by ratios. For example, if Ted Williams' batting average was 350 for the first half of the year and 381 for the second half, one might imagine that his average for the whole season might be $\frac{350+381}{2} = 366$. To calculate his actual batting average, the ratios of hits to times-at-bat for each half need to be combined into a new ratio and the subsequent decimal computed. For example, if the first-half batting average ratio of $\frac{70}{200} = 0.350$ and the

second-half average of $\frac{8}{21} = 0.381$, then the overall season batting average is $\frac{78}{221} = 0.353$, not 0.366. Note that the overall ratio is weighted by the large number of times at bat during the first half of the season. (Williams may have had an injury the second half of the season, for example.)

In fact, this procedure helps explain the following paradox. Suppose Babe Ruth had a batting average ratio of $\frac{17}{50} = 0.340$ for the first half of the season and $\frac{55}{150} = 0.367$ for the second half. Note that his batting average is lower than Williams' for both halves of the season. However, Ruth's overall batting-average ratio would be $\frac{72}{200} = 0.360$, which is *higher* than Williams' season average!

Investigation One

Tournaments

1 The people who make schedules for hockey, soccer, tennis, and other games use some special—and strange-sounding—words!

- When setting up a series of games among several teams, the tournament master establishes a *draw*. That means he or she selects which teams will play against each other in each round.

- A *round-robin* draw pairs teams in several rounds so that each team plays every other team only once.

- If a team doesn't play in a round, it has been assigned a *bye*.

This table shows the draw for a hockey round-robin tournament. In round 1, A v B and C v D. (A v B means "Team A versus Team B.")

v	A	B	C	D
A		1	2	3
B	1		3	2
C	2	3		1
D	3	2	1	

a This draw won't work. Explain why.

b Ronnie is asked to make a correct draw that allows every team to play every other team. She begins by looking at a simpler problem with only two teams. Then she looks at the problem with three teams.

i Why are there no numbers in the squares along the diagonal?

v	A	B
A		1
B	1	

ii Complete the following tables for three teams.

v	A	B	C
A		1	2
B	1		
C	2		

Round 1	Round 2	Round 3
A v B	A v C	

iii What happens to team C in round 1?

c i Complete Ronnie's draw for a four-team round robin.

v	A	B	C	D
A		1	2	
B	1		3	
C	2			
D				

ii Is Ronnie's completed table symmetrical? Explain your answer.

d Here is part of Ronnie's table for a six-team round-robin tournament.

v	A	B	C	D	E	F
A		1	2	3	4	5
B	1		3	4	5	
C	2					
D	3					
E	4					
F	5					

i   Do you think her completed table will be symmetrical? Explain your answer.

ii   Complete the six-team table.

iii   Use your completed table to help complete the following table.

Round 1	Round 2	Round 3	Round 4	Round 5
A ∨ B	A ∨ C			

e   Use Ronnie's method to make round-robin draws for:

   i   eight teams.

   ii   ten teams.

2   Seven teams enter a hockey round-robin tournament.

   a   Find a way of using Ronnie's method in **1** to make the draw.

   b   Explain how to make a round-robin draw for any odd number of teams.

3   The table on the next page shows the results of a basketball league. Each team plays every other team just once. Points are awarded as shown in the box:

> *Win* — 4 points
>
> *Tie* — 2 points
>
> *Loss by 6 goals or less* — 1 point
>
> *Loss by 7 goals or more* — 0 points

Team	Points
Las Vegas	40
Espanola	36
Dixon	31
Taos	25
Cimarron	22
Eagle Nest	16
Los Alamos	15
Alameda	13
Santa Fe	13
Willard	12
Belen	8
Total	231

a Complete each table for games played in round-robin competitions with two teams, three teams, and four teams.

v	A	B
A		
B		

Number of games played: _____

v	A	B	C
A			
B			
C			

Number of games played: _____

v	A	B	C	D
A				
B				
C				
D				

Number of games played: _____

b By looking for a pattern in **a**, work out the number of games in the basketball league of eleven teams.

c Complete the following table.

Number of Teams	Number of Games Played by Each Team	Total Number of Games Played
2	1	1
3	2	3
4	3	
5		
11		

d How many games would be played in a competition with *n* teams? Explain your formula.

e i Explain why at least 220 points are awarded in an eleven-team competition.

  ii How many games were lost by a margin of six goals or less in this basketball-league competition?

f There are 21 teams in the Eastern Division Soccer League. Each team plays every other team at home *and* away. There are two complete round-robins. How many games are played:

  i in the first round?

  ii in total?

g Suppose there are *n* teams in the league. Can you write a formula that tells how many games will be played at home and away in a round-robin competition?

4 The Five Nations Rugby Championship is played each year. Teams get two points for each game they win.

a Who won the championship shown in this diagram?

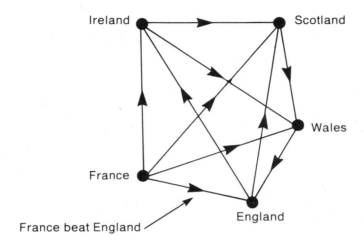

France beat England

b John thinks he remembers that *all* five nations shared the championship in 1983. There were no draws, and every team earned the same number of points. Draw a diagram to show why John might be correct.

c Four basketball teams—Canada (C), England (E), United States (US), and New Zealand (NZ)—play each other once. They earn points according to the following chart.

> *Win* — 2 points
> *Loss*— 0 points
> *Tie* — play extra time to find a winner

Use this diagram to show the United States and New Zealand sharing the championship.

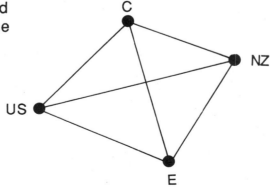

d **i** How many points in total are awarded in the basketball championship?

    ii Show that the tournament *cannot* end with all four teams having the same number of points.

e Suppose seven international basketball teams enter the competition instead of four.

    i How many points are awarded?

    ii Can all seven teams, in theory, win the same number of points and share the championship?

f Repeat **e** for:

    i eight teams.

    ii nine teams.

    iii *n* teams (when *n* is odd).

    iv *n* teams (when *n* is even).

ON YOUR OWN

In the event of a tie at the end of a game, find out the various ways people in different sports decide the winner.

5 Thirty-two players enter the World Racketball Championship.
A typical *elimination* draw for four players is shown below.
(An elimination draw means losers are eliminated from the
tournament.)

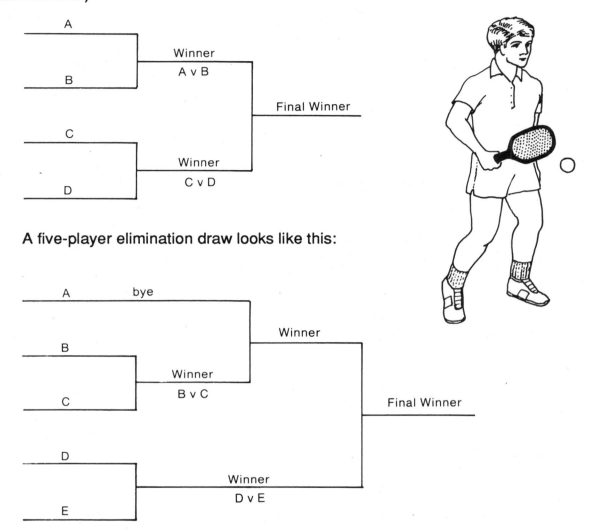

A five-player elimination draw looks like this:

a How many games in total will be played before the winner of the
World Championship is found? (Hint: Try solving a set of simpler
problems first and look for a pattern.)

b If an elimination championship has *n* players, how many games
must be played?

c The tournament organizers decide to place the top eight—or
seeded—players into round 2. They allow 48 players into round 1
(56 players in all). How many total games will be played to find the
championship winner?

d A *double elimination* tournament means that a player must lose *twice* to be eliminated. What is the maximum number of games needed for a five-player double-elimination tournament? For *n* teams?

*O*N YOUR OWN

There are three soccer divisions for different-sized high schools. Division *A* is for schools with 1,500–2,000 students, Division *B* for schools with 800–1,499 students, and Division *C* for schools with less than 800 students. The top five teams in each division compete in a final tournament. To keep the tournament interesting, the organizers arrange an elimination draw in which Division *C* teams play each other for the first two rounds and then Divisions *A* and *B* join in at round 3. How many games must be played to find a winner? Also, why did the organizers decide to let only Division *C* teams play the first rounds?

6 In the 1990 World Soccer Cup tournament, 24 teams played in six groups in round-robin competitions. The top two teams in each group, along with the next best four teams, then advanced to Stage 2 (making sixteen teams in all).

Stage 2 was an elimination competition. How many games were played during the complete World Cup competition?

7 In a chess championship, sixteen chess masters played against each other in four groups. The competition for each group was a round robin. The top two players in each group advanced to Stage 2, which was an elimination competition.

a How many games in all were played during the competition?

b The average attendance for each game was estimated at 650 people. What was the total attendance for the chess matches?

Investigation Two

Systematic Counting

1 a A final score of 1 point is not possible in football. Why not?

   b Which final point totals are impossible in football?

   c Huey claims his team scored 8 points from a touchdown and two points-after. Is this possible?

Football Scoring

T = touchdown	6 points
F = field goal	3 points
S = safety	2 points
P = point-after	1 point

---

   d Systematically fill in the table to show all the ways of scoring 12 points. (Remember that you must have a touchdown to try for a point-after.)

T	F	S	P	Total
2	0	0	0	12
1	2	0	0	12
1	1	1	1	12

2 a During a recent football game, the Giants scored 18 points. Complete the table systematically to find all the ways of scoring 18 points.

T	F	S	P	Total
3	0	0	0	18
2	2	0	0	18
2	1	1	1	18
2	0	2	2	18

b Make a table to find all the ways of scoring 19 points.

3 The following two scoring systems A and B are used to award team points during the annual school sports day.

System A
First place — 4 points
Second place — 3 points

System B
First place — 5 points
Second place — 2 points

a Red Team finished the day with 24 points awarded under System A.

Find all the ways Red Team could have gained its points. You may want to make a table to find the possibilities.

b Using System B, Red Team's points only would have been 23. Find all the possible ways of gaining 23 points under System B.

c How many firsts and how many seconds did Red Team actually get during the sports day?

4 The table shows how points are awarded in Rugby League and Rugby Union, two versions of the same game. A *try* is similar to a touchdown in football; a *conversion* is like the point-after in football; a *penalty goal* is scored from a free kick through the goal posts after a penalty; and a *dropped goal* is scored during play when the ball is dropped from the hands and drop-kicked over the crossbar between the goal posts.

	Rugby League	Rugby Union
Try	4	4
Conversion	2	2
Penalty Goal	2	3
Dropped Goal	1	3

In a Rugby League match, the Green Team scored 13 points. Under the Rugby Union scoring system, they would have scored 16 points. How did the Green Team score their points?

5 Using the new scoring system in soccer, Mt. Washington School has 21 points after eleven games.

	New points	Old points
Win	3	2
Tie	1	1
Loss	0	0

Under the old system, the team would have had 15 points. How many games did Mt. Washington:

a win?

b tie?

c lose?

6 The All-Star Basketball Team scored 24 points by the first time-out. If the team scored eight 1-pointers, how many 2-pointers and 3-pointers did they score? Give all possible answers.

NBA Basketball Scoring

3 points— basket scored from outside the 23-foot line.
2 points— basket scored from inside the 23-foot line.
1 point— basket scored on a free shot after a penalty.

7 Four women's hockey teams play each other in a round-robin competition.

	Win	Tie	Loss	Total For	Goals Against
United States	2	0	1	5	1
Canada	2	0	1	3	5
New Zealand	1	0	2	5	6
Soviet Union	1	0	2	4	5

If no two games had the same score, what was the score between the United States and the Soviet Union?

8 In a shooting match, three shooters— Pedro, Kyla, and Maureen—each scored 71 points with six shots. They all hit the target every time. Pedro's first two shots were awarded 22 points, while Kyla's first shot produced only 3 points. Who hit the bull's eye? Explain your answer.

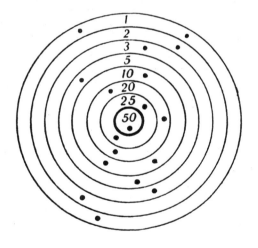

Hint: Study the picture of the target carefully. Note how many holes are in each ring of the target.

Investigation Three

Using Rates

1 The chicken and the rabbit have a race around a 400-meter running track. The race is 800 meters (or two laps) long. The chicken can maintain a top speed of 4 meters per second, so the rabbit agrees to run the first lap at 10 meters per second—then to slow to 2 meters per second for the last lap.

a The rabbit assumes that his average speed is 6 meters per second $\left(\dfrac{10+2}{2}\right)$ so he will easily win. Do you think he is correct ? Explain your answer.

	Speed	
	Chicken	**Rabbit**
Lap 1	4 m/s	10 m/s
Lap 2	4 m/s	2 m/s

b i Complete this table.

	Time (seconds)	
	Chicken	**Rabbit**
Lap 1	100	40
Lap 2		
Totals		

ii Show that the rabbit's average speed for the race is 3.3 m/s (to the nearest tenth).

iii Who wins the race?

c   Explain why the rabbit will win if he runs the first lap at 10 m/s and the second at any speed faster than 2.5 m/s.

d   Complete the table for the rabbit.

Speed (m/s)		Time (s)		Total Time (s)	Average Speed of Rabbit (m/s to nearest tenth)
Lap 1	Lap 2	Lap 1	Lap2		
20	10				
5	20				
8	10				
10	2				
1	20				

2   Cathy and Dan each drive a car 280 miles from Seattle to Spokane. Cathy drives at a steady speed of 50 miles per hour. Dan is tired, so he deliberately drives at 40 miles per hour for the first 120 miles. What is the minimum speed Dan must go for the remaining 160 miles to beat Cathy to Spokane?

3   When training on a 400-meter track, Marilyn does three laps at 6 m/s and one additional lap at 8 m/s.

a   Predict whether her average speed over four laps will be closer to 6 m/s or 8 m/s. Explain your answer.

b   How long does it take to run:

   i   the first three laps?

   ii   the last lap?

c   What is Marilyn's average speed?

d   The next day she runs one lap at 5 m/s, three laps at 6 m/s, then two laps at 8 m/s. Find her average speed.

e   Suppose the track was actually 400.61 meters long. Would this alter your answers to c and d? Explain your answer.

4   Sensitive computer equipment is used to measure the time it takes the lead cyclist in a triathlon to cover the distance of five feet between the two sensor pads on the road.

a   The lead cyclist covers the five feet in 0.1000 second, and the equipment records the speed between the pads as 34.09 miles per hour.

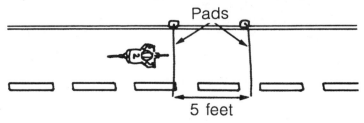

    i How far does the cyclist move in 1 second? In 1 hour?

    ii Explain why the speed-sensor computer has correctly calculated the speed of the bicycle.

b Sensor pads are sometimes used by the highway patrol to detect speeding drivers.

	Speed limits
Town	30 mph
Highway	55 mph

A car takes 0.0652 of a second to move between pads that are five feet apart. Will the driver receive a speeding ticket:

    i in town?

    ii on the highway?

ON YOUR OWN

Suppose you run the first lap of a race at a speed of x meters per second and the second lap at y meters per second. Use examples to show that your average speed for the whole race is $\dfrac{x+y}{2}$ m/s *only* when $x = y$—that is, when both laps are run at the same speed.

5 In the first 11 games of the 12-game National Women's Softball Tournament, Rita reaches first base 14 times in 29 turns at bat.

    a i Explain why her batting average is 0.483. (Sometimes people say a batting average is "483," although they really mean 483 *thousandths*.)

    ii Is this a high average in world-class softball? How does it compare with professional baseball batting averages?

    b In the last game, Rita gets two hits out of three turns at bat. Show that her overall tournament batting average is 0.500.

6 Suppose Ted Williams got 70 hits out of 200 times at bat during the first half-year of the season and 8 hits out of 21 times at bat during the second half.

  a What was his batting average for:

  i the first half of the season?

  ii the second half of the season?

  iii the whole season?

  iv Does the *average* of the two half-season batting averages equal the result in **iii**? Explain your answer.

  b Suppose Babe Ruth got 17 hits out of 50 times at bat during the first half and 55 hits out of 150 times at bat the second half of the season. What was his batting average for:

  i the first half of the season?

  ii the second half of the season?

  iii the whole season?

  iv Does the average of the two half-season batting averages equal the result in **iii**? Explain your answer.

  c Compare the batting statistics for Williams and Ruth.

  i Who had a higher batting average in the first half of the season? In the second half?

  ii Who had the higher overall season batting average? Explain your answer.

CHECK-UP

1 This table shows the pre-tournament ranking, or *seeding,* of teams in a women's tennis tournament. To ensure a high level of interest throughout the round-robin tournament, the organizers plan for the Chandler-Northcote clash to be in the final round. In addition, Albion will play Omega in the first round.

Team	Seed
Chandler (C)	1
Northcote (N)	2
Walgett (W)	3
Albion (A)	4
Omega (O)	5

Complete the five-round tournament draw table.

Round 1	Round 2	Round 3	Round 4	Round 5
A v O				C v N

2 In a modified form of football, points are awarded only for touchdowns and field goals. There are no points-after or safeties.

> *Touchdown* – 7 points
> *Field goal* – 4 points

a How many ways are there of scoring 27 points?

b What scores cannot be achieved in this game?

3 Christine plans her split-times for a marathon (26.2 miles) according to the table. In what total time does she expect to complete the marathon?

Splits (miles)	Average rate (minutes/mile)
0 – 6	6.6
6 – 12	5.8
12 – 18	5.3
18 – 21	6.6
21 – 26.2	6.3

4 The table shows the goals scored by the four top basketball players in a team during a tournament. Complete this table.

Name	Goals scored	Games played	Goals/game
Margaret		5	20
Rhonda	84	4	
Susan		2	28
Kay	120		24
Totals	360	16	

DISCOVERING RULES

TEACHING NOTES

Relationships found in physics, geometry, and other real-world situations often can be expressed as rules in the form of equations. While it is relatively easy to calculate specific values that satisfy a given equation (that is, for $2x = y$, if $x = 1$, then $y = 2$, and so on), finding an equation that consistently represents a set of coordinate values is a much more difficult problem. For example, what equation represents the following set of *(x,y)* values?

$$(0, ^-1), (1, 1), (2, 3), (3, 5), (4, 7), (5, 9)$$

The process of *finite differences* provides a systematic method for finding the coefficients for polynomials that represent differents sets of (x,y) values. To use this method, first organize the (x,y) pairs in a table and find the difference between the sequential pairs of y values. Do you find a constant difference? If not, continue to subtract successive differences until a constant difference appears.

Here is a table of the (x,y) values from above and their differences.

x	y	Difference
0	$^-1$	
		2
1	1	
		2
2	3	
		2
3	5	
		2
4	7	
		2
5	9	

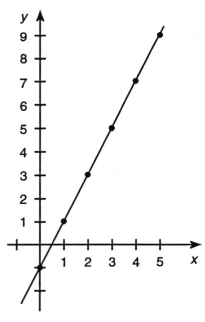

Plotting the (x,y) pairs shows that they are *collinear* meaning they are all points that lie on a single line. A *linear equation* of the form $y = ax + b$ can describe them.

The constant difference from the table is the value of *a,* the *slope* of the line passing through the points.

$$\text{Slope} = \frac{y_2 - y_1}{x_2 - x_1}$$

where (x_1, y_1) and (x_2, y_2) are any two points on the line. For the (x, y) values in our table, the difference between successive x values is always 1. The difference between y values is the constant difference in the table, so

$$a = \frac{2}{1}$$

Now find b: It is the y value when $x = 0$ or $a(0) + b = {}^-1$. Since we know the values of a and b, we can determine the rule for the set of points in the table. It is the linear equation $y = 2x - 1$, which describes the line plotted from the points above.

If a table of values requires two differences before you find a constant, the resulting equation will be *quadratic*. Similarly, third-degree (*cubic*) equations result from tables that require three differences to find a constant; fourth-degree, four differences; and so on. The chart of general equations on p. 49 summarizes the finite-differences process for first-degree through fourth-degree polynomials. You may want to photocopy this chart for your students. In most of the investigations in this chapter, students use the finite-differences process to discover the rule for a given set of points—usually in the context of a real-world situation. The following example demonstrates the steps students take to solve such a problem.

Sample Problem: Find a rule that describes these points:
(0, 3), (1, 9), (2, 19), (3, 33), (4, 51), (5, 73)

Solution: Organize the (x, y) values in a table and use the finite-differences process to find a constant difference:

x	y	First Difference	Second Difference
0	3		
		6	
1	9		4
		10	
2	19		4
		14	
3	33		4
		18	
4	51		4
		22	
5	73		

Since this table requires two differences to find a constant, the resulting equation is quadratic: It can be written in the form of $ax^2 + bx + c = y$. If students use the chart on p. 49, they'll find that

$$2a = 4, \text{ so } a = 2$$
$$a + b = 6, \text{ so } b = 4$$
$$c = 3$$

Therefore, $2x^2 + 4x + 3 = y$ is the rule that describes the given set of points.

Be careful when the table of values does not begin with $x = 0$. You may want to discuss with students how to proceed when a problem is presented this way. They should either use the difference patterns to extend the table to include the $x = 0$ case or refer to the chart of general equations on p. 49 to derive a specific rule.

For example, Investigation Two contains a problem in which students discover a rule for how long it takes to cook a turkey depending on its weight. The table of (x, y) values starts at x (weight) = 1. Students can extend the difference table to $x = 0$ to find a rule. However, in the real world it doesn't make sense to create a table of values in which the weight of a turkey is zero. In this problem, using the chart of general equations to discover a rule may be a better procedure.

Ask students to think about when it's appropriate to use a mathematical process to represent a real-world situation—and when the process may break down. Discussing how—and when—to use a process such as the finite-differences method can encourage students to make meaningful connections between the world they live in and mathematics. A simple computer spreadsheet constructed to automatically calculate the difference columns can be a useful instructional tool.

Note: Keep in mind that tables representing exponential patterns will never produce a constant using the finite-difference method; therefore, the procedure will not help find such equations. The following table shows the pattern of differences for the exponential equation $2^x = y$:

x	y	First Difference	Second Difference
0	1		
		1	
1	2		1
		2	
2	4		2
		4	
3	8		4
		8	
4	16		8
		16	
5	32		

Investigation One • Rules from Geometric Patterns

The first series of problems asks students to discover a rule that relates two sets of objects—without introducing the finite-differences technique. The rules for the problems in this investigation are discovered by drawing a geometric pattern and noting the relationship as the pattern grows by one unit at a time. In the first problem, students design a rule to predict the number of rails (r) in a fence if the number of posts (p) is known: $r = 4(p - 1)$. Students often mistakenly assume that there will be four times as many rails as posts—but the rule needs to take into account the first (or last) pole in the fence. The construction of a bridge, matchstick figures, paving-stone patterns, molecular structures, and other situations are also explored.

Investigation Two • Discovering Linear Rules

This investigation introduces the *finite-differences* procedure for linear equations. Using salary rates, exercise programs, two-dimensional construction projects, and other rate problems, students develop a two-column table, calculate the differences in pairs of y values, and use the constant to write an appropriate equation in the form $ax + b = y$. Students also explore the relationships between the table values, a and b in the equation for a line, and the physical characteristics of the line passing through the points.

Investigation Three • Discovering Quadratic Rules

Students extend the finite-differences procedure to quadratic relationships. Situations include stacking dominos and cards, handshakes, geometric constructions, and other problems that explore tables of relationships which require two differences to arrive at a constant. Such relationships are described by equations in the form $ax^2 + bx + c = y$.

Investigation Four • Exploring More Complex Rules

Students extend the finite-differences procedure to third-degree and fourth-degree relationships. Situations include stacking fruit, geometric constructions, and other problems that explore tables of relationships which require three differences to arrive at a constant. Such relationships are described by equations in the form $ax^3 + bx^2 + cx + d = y$ and $ax^4 + bx^3 + cx^2 + dx + e = y$.

CHART OF GENERAL EQUATIONS

First Degree

$y = ax + b$

x	y	
0	b	
		$> a$
1	$a + b$	
		$> a$
2	$2a + b$	
		$> a$
3	$3a + b$	
		$> a$
4	$4a + b$	
		$> a$
5	$5a + b$	

Second Degree

$y = ax^2 + bx + c$

x	y		
0	c		
		$> a + b$	
1	$a + b + c$		$> 2a$
		$> 3a + b$	
2	$4a + 2b + c$		$> 2a$
		$> 5a + b$	
3	$9a + 3b + c$		$> 2a$
		$> 7a + b$	
4	$16a + 4b + c$		$> 2a$
		$> 9a + b$	
5	$25a + 5b + c$		

Third Degree

$y = ax^3 + bx^2 + cx + d$

x	y			
0	d			
		$> a + b + c$		
1	$a + b + c + d$		$> 6a + 2b$	
		$> 7a + 3b + c$		$> 6a$
2	$8a + 4b + 2c + d$		$> 12a + 2b$	
		$> 19a + 5b + c$		$> 6a$
3	$27a + 9b + 3c + d$		$> 18a + 2b$	
		$> 37a + 7b + c$		$> 6a$
4	$64a + 16b + 4c + d$		$> 24a + 2b$	
		$> 61a + 9b + c$		
5	$125a + 25b + 5c + d$			

Fourth Degree

$y = ax^4 + bx^3 + cx^2 + dx + e$

x	y				
0	e				
		$> a + b + c + d$			
1	$a + b + c + d + e$		$> 14a + 6b + 2c$		
		$> 15a + 7b + 3c + d$		$> 36a + 6b$	
2	$16a + 8b + 4c + 2d + e$		$> 50a + 12b + 2c$		$> 24a$
		$> 65a + 19b + 5c + d$		$> 60a + 6b$	
3	$81a + 27b + 9c + 3d + e$		$> 110a + 18b + 2c$		$> 24a$
		$> 175a + 37b + 7c + d$		$> 84a + 6b$	
4	$256a + 64b + 16c + 4d + e$		$> 194a + 24b + 2c$		$> 24a$
		$> 369a + 61b + 9c + d$		$> 108a + 6b$	
5	$625a + 125b + 25c + 5d + e$		$> 302a + 30b + 2c$		
		$> 671a + 91b + 11c + d$			
6	$1296a + 216b + 36c + 6d + e$				

Investigation One

Rules from Geometric Patterns

1 Slim designs a fence around his ranch. The fence keeps unwanted animals out. There is also a cattle guard constructed from a grid of steel pipe over a hole in the ground where the road passes through the fence.

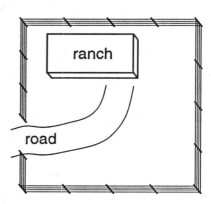

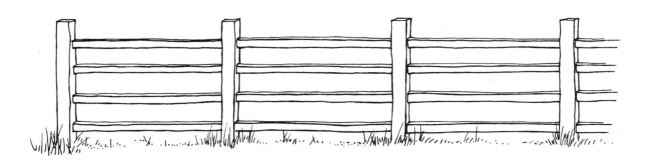

Slim wants a rule relating *p,* the number of posts in the fence, to *r,* the number of rails.

a Can you discover a rule that works for any length of fence?

b Slim decides that the basic unit of his design looks like this:

He adds one unit for every extra post. For *p* = 3 he makes the following sketch:

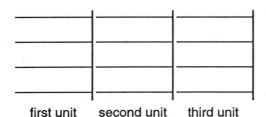

first unit   second unit   third unit

5 Make a sketch showing a pattern to explain why Slim's formula is $r = 4p - 4$. Why do you need to subtract 4 to get the correct number of rails?

c Slim claims that $r = 4 \times (p - 1)$ is also correct.

   i Is he right?

   ii Does your pattern in **b** justify this rule, too?

d If $p = 18$, how many rails does Slim need?

2 One side of a long bridge is constructed of triangles made from steel girders (g) of equal length.

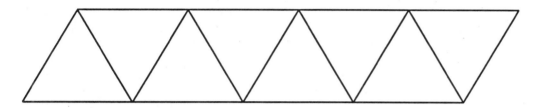

Laurie wants to find a formula for the number of girders (g) needed to make a side with n triangles.

She decides to use as the basic unit.

    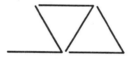

   $n = 1$ $n = 2$ $n = 3$

a Draw a diagram for $n = 4$.

b Laurie notices a geometrical pattern and writes $g = 2n + 1$. Explain her reasoning.

c Use Laurie's method to find a rule for the number of matchsticks required in each of the following patterns:

   i

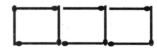

          Hint: Use as the basic unit.

   ii

---

iii

 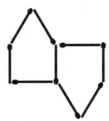 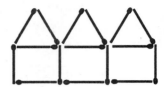

iv

 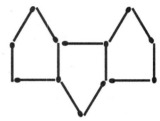

v

  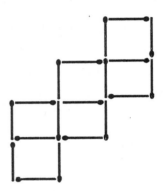

d Matchstick patterns are made by using regular *n*-gons: *n* = the number of sides, and *x* = the number of each basic shape used.

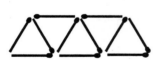  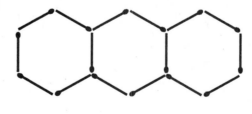

$n = 3$
$x = 5$

$n = 5$
$x = 2$

$n = 6$
$x = 3$

Can you find *one* formula for the number of matches (*m*) needed to make a shape with regular *n*-gons?

3 In the following design, hexagonal gardens are surrounded by hexagonal paving stones.

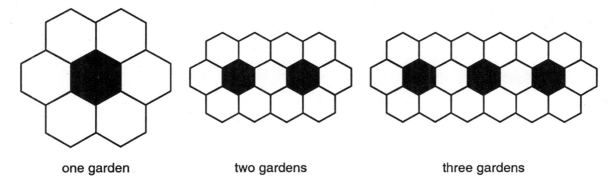

one garden   two gardens   three gardens

a Find a rule or formula for *x* gardens and *y* paving stones.

b Can you justify the rule using only the geometric design?

c How many paving stones do you need for 10 gardens?

4 These diagrams show the molecular structure for a class of hydrocarbons called the *alkanes*.

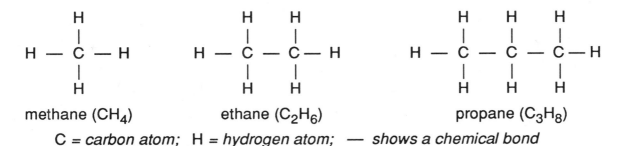

methane (CH_4)   ethane (C_2H_6)   propane (C_3H_8)

C = *carbon atom;* H = *hydrogen atom;* — *shows a chemical bond*

a Draw diagrams for pentane (five carbon atoms) and hexane (six carbon atoms).

b Caroline uses
$$
\begin{array}{c}
\text{H} \\
| \\
\text{C} \\
| \\
\text{H}
\end{array}
$$
as her basic unit.

Suppose **we** write the formula for alkanes C_nH_m. Explain why Caroline thinks C_nH_{2n+2} is the *general-class* formula for alkanes. In other words, why does she think $m = 2n + 2$?

c Hectane has 100 carbon atoms. How many hydrogen atoms does it have?

d Here are the first three of the class of hydrocarbons called the *alkenes*. (Note that this class of chemicals is different from alkanes.)

$$H_2C = CH - H$$

(The structural diagrams, left to right:)

ethene (C_2H_4)   propene (C_3H_6)   butene (C_4H_8)

= *shows a double chemical bond*

i   Draw diagrams for pentene (five carbon atoms) and hexene (six carbon atoms).

ii   If the formula for alkenes is C_nH_m, find a rule relating n and m.

e   The first few *alkynes* are shown in the following diagrams:

ethyne (C_2H_2)   propyne (C_3H_4)   butyne (C_4H_6)

≡ *shows a triple chemical bond*

If C_nH_m is the alkyne formula, write a rule that relates m and n.

ON YOUR OWN

Look in an encyclopedia or chemistry textbook and find out about the following classes of organic chemicals. Devise a general-class formula for each.

1   alcohol   2   aldehydes   3   fatty acids

5   A basketball league has 18 teams. Each team plays every other team twice, once at home and once away. A sponsor offers $10,000 for each game but wants to know how much the sponsorship will cost. The sponsor prepares a set of tables to figure out the number of games for the teams in a league.

n	=	the number of teams in a league
g	=	the number of games
✔	=	a game is played
✗	=	no game is played

$n = 2$

V	A	B
A	✗	✔
B	✔	✗

$g = 2$

$n = 3$

V	A	B	C
A	✗	✔	✔
B	✔	✗	✔
C	✔	✔	✗

$g = 6$

$n = 4$

V	A	B	C	D
A	✗	✔	✔	✔
B	✔	✗	✔	✔
C	✔	✔	✗	✔
D	✔	✔	✔	✗

$g = 12$

a i The sponsor notices a geometrical pattern in the tables. He uses the pattern to reason that in an 18-team league there will be 18×17 games. Explain this reasoning. Is he correct?

  ii How much will the sponsorship of 18 teams cost?

b Another geometrical pattern for the sponsorship leads to the formula: $(18 \times 18) - 18$ games. Is this formula also correct? Explain your reasoning.

c Find two general formulas linking g and n that use the patterns discussed in **a** and **b**.

6 A gardener designs square gardens with a square planting area in the middle. Each square garden has *x* tiles on each side. *y* = the total number of tiles needed. The gardener needs a formula that relates *y* and *x*, so she draws the first few gardens:

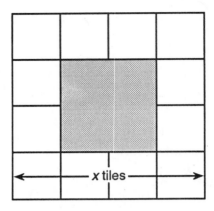

x = 3

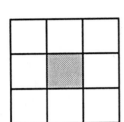

y = 8

x = 4

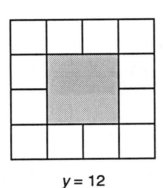

y = 12

x = 5

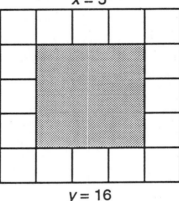

y = 16

a Find a formula that relates *x* and *y*.

b i Explain why $y = x^2 - (x - 2)^2$

ii Does the result in **i** agree with your formula in **a**?

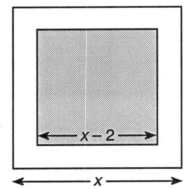

c Use the geometric design to the right to help explain why $y = 2x + 2(x - 2)$.

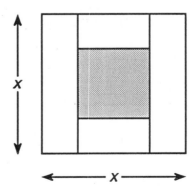

d Use these results to show that:
$$x^2 - (x - 2)^2 = 4x - 4 = 2x + 2(x - 2).$$

7 Jenny wants to draw this *mystic rose* for a math-art competition.

She wonders how many lines (chords) she will have to draw.

a Jenny focuses on one point, P, and notices that 19 lines start there.

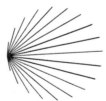

She reasons that for 3 points there will be 3×2 lines, and for 4 points there will be 4×3 lines. Make sketches for 5, 6, and 7 points to check her reasoning. Is she correct?

b Since there are 20 points in her mystic rose, she predicts there must be 20 × 19 lines. However, there are *not* 20 × 19 lines for a 20-point mystic rose. How many are there?

c How many lines will an *n*-point mystic rose have?

Investigation Two

Discovering Linear Rules

1 A plumber charges $y for x hours of work.

> ### Plumber's Rates
> **$50 home-visit charge**
> **plus**
> **$25 per hour**

a Explain why $y = 25x + 50$.

b The plumber arrives at a job only to find that the repairs have already been done.

   i What does the plumber charge?

   ii Is this charge fair? Explain your answer.

c Explain how the formula $y = 25x + 50$ is represented by this table.

x	y	Difference
0	50	
		25
1	75	
		25
2	100	
		25
3	125	
		25
4	150	

d The following table shows how much an electrician charges. y is the charge for x hours of labor.

x	y	Difference
0	40	
		30
1	70	
		☐
2	100	
		☐
3	130	
		☐
4	160	

i Write the missing differences in the table.

ii Use the table to write a formula for the electrician's labor charges.

iii Make an advertisement for the electrician's charges.

2 Write the formula for each of the following tables. Check each formula by substituting each x value in the table to see if it gives the corresponding y value for all *(x,y)* pairs.

a

x	y	Difference
0	1	
		☐
1	6	
		☐
2	11	
		☐
3	16	

b

x	y	Difference
0	2	
		☐
1	6	
		☐
2	10	
		☐
3	14	

c

x	y	Difference
0	2	
		☐
1	2.5	
		☐
2	3	
		☐
3	3.5	

d

x	y	Difference
0	2	
		☐
1	2.2	
		☐
2	2.4	
		☐
3	2.6	

e

x	y	Difference
0	10	☐
1	20	☐
2	30	☐
3	40	

f

x	y	Difference
0	c	☐
1	$m + c$	☐
2	$2m + c$	☐
3	$3m + c$	

3 This table shows cooking times for turkeys weighing up to 5 kilograms. *w* represents the weight of a turkey, and *t* is the number of minutes it takes to cook.

w	t
1	45
2	75
3	105
4	135
5	165

Dale notices there is a constant-difference pattern of 30 minutes. He writes a cooking formula:

$$t = 30w + 45$$

a Is Dale's formula correct?

b **i** Dale prepares another table. What number should go in the box?

    ii Write the correct formula.

    iii Explain why $w = 0$ does not really make sense in this situation.

w	t	Difference
0	☐	
		30
1	45	
		30
2	75	
		30
3	105	
		30
4	135	
		30
5	165	

c The formula for this problem fits the general equation $y = ax + b$. Here is a table of differences for the general equation:

x	y	Difference
0	b	
		a
1	a + b	
		a
2	2a + b	
		a
3	3a + b	
		a
4	4a + b	
		a
5	5a + b	

Dale wants to find the correct formula without adding $w = 0$ to his table. He uses the table of differences for the general equation. Explain how he does this.

4 Mary wants to get in better shape gradually. She does 9 situps the first week, 13 situps the second week, then 17, 21, and so on. Her sequence of situps is 9, 13, 17, 21, ⋯ .

a Complete the table to find a formula that gives *s:* the number of situps Mary does in her n^{th} week of getting in shape.

Week	Situps	Difference
0	☐	
		☐
1	9	
		☐
2	13	
		☐
3	17	
		☐
4	21	
⋮	⋮	
n	☐	

b In which week does she complete:

   i 101 situps?

   ii 89 situps?

   iii 61 situps?

   iv What does "Week 0" describe in this situation?

c Find the rules for the nth term in the following sequences:

   i 2, 8, 14, 20, ⋯

   ii 1, 11, 21, 31, ⋯

   iii 1.1, 1.2, 1.3, 1.4, ⋯

   iv 16, 14, 12, 10, ⋯

   v 100, 97, 94, 91, ⋯

   vi $a, a + d, a + 2d, a + 3d, \cdots$

5 A contractor lays square concrete tiles to make a supermarket parking lot 99 units by 98 units. Each tile has an area of 1 unit². A worker accidentally drives a bulldozer diagonally from A to B, breaking all the tiles it touches. Each broken tile costs $10 to replace. The contractor needs to work out the cost of replacing the broken tiles.

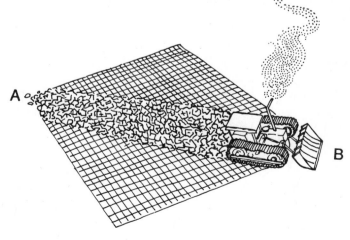

a The contractor draws a series of parking lots with length *x* units and width (*x* – 1) units. The number of broken (shaded) tiles is *y*.

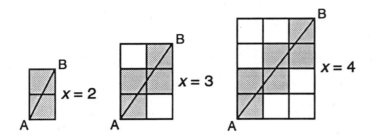

   i Draw the rectangle for *x* = 5.

   ii Prepare a difference table and use it to find a formula for *y* in terms of *x* .

b **i** How many tiles did the worker break?

   ii What was the cost of repairs?

ON YOUR OWN

In problem **5**, suppose the parking lot was *x* units by (*x* – 2) units. Find a rule for the number of tiles the worker would break in going diagonally from A to B. Then work out a general rule for broken tiles that result from driving diagonally from A to B in *any* rectangular parking lot.

6 Ben makes rose gardens with the width 1 unit less than the length. Each garden measures *x* units by (*x* + 1) units, where *x* is a whole number. The rectangular gardens are surrounded by square paving stones.

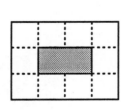
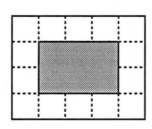
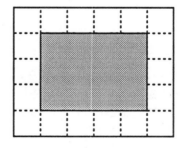

      x = 1   *x* = 2   *x* = 3
      y = 2   *y* = 3   *y* = 4
      t = 10   *t* = 14   *t* = 18

a i Find a formula that relates the width of the garden (x) and the number of paving stones (t) needed to surround the garden.

ii If the garden measures 99 × 100, how many paving stones are needed?

b Try phrasing the problem in a different way: Ben's gardens have a length of y units and a width of $y - 1$ units.

i Find a formula that gives the number of paving stones (t) needed to surround the garden with a length of y.

ii If this type of garden measures 99 x 100, how many paving stones are needed to surround the garden?

c Compare your answers in **a ii** and **b ii**.

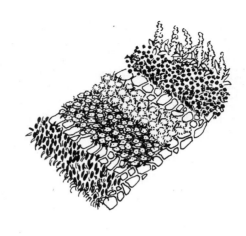

7 All the problems you've solved so far in this investigation require only one step to arrive at a constant difference. Formulas that match $y = ax + b$ are called *linear equations*. That's because the graph of the (x,y) pairs form a straight line—such as the diagonal of broken tiles created by the bulldozer. Try graphing the (x,y) pairs from any of the previous problems on a coordinate plane for other examples.

Suppose the third and fourth terms of a linear sequence are 16 and 21:

n	n^{th} Term	Difference
0	☐	
		☐
1	☐	
		☐
2	☐	
		☐
3	16	
		☐
4	21	
⋮	⋮	
n	☐	

a Find a formula for the nth term of the sequence. Then graph the sequence.

b The second and fifth terms of a linear sequence are 4 and 13. Construct a difference table and find a formula for the nth term. Graph the sequence.

8 Lucy, an Olympic sprinter, runs an average speed of 9 meters/second in a 100-meter race.

Her young son Gary runs an average speed of 5 meters/second in a 100-meter race.

When mother and son compete in a 100-meter race, Lucy gives Gary a 50-meter head start.

a **i** Use the difference tables for Lucy and Gary to find formulas that relate distance (d) and time (t).

LUCY

t	d	Difference
0	0	
		☐
1	9	
		☐
2	18	
		☐
3	☐	

GARY

t	d	Difference
0	50	
		☐
1	55	
		☐
2	☐	
		☐
3	☐	

    ii Write a short paragraph that explains each formula in terms of average speed and starting position.

b The line graphs below show Lucy's and Gary's distance for each second of the race.

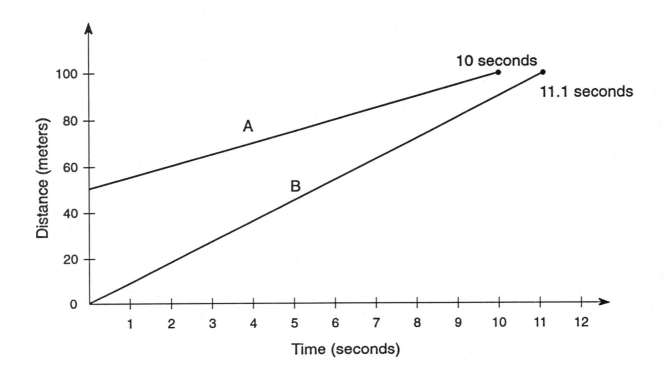

    i Which line graph (A or B) represents Gary?

    ii Use the graph to explain who won the race.

c In reality, the graphs of a foot race will not be exactly linear. Why not?

9 The graphs on the next page show the television rental charges for two companies, *TeleHire* and *TeleRent*.

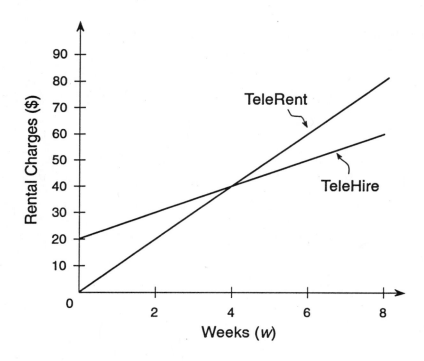

a Which company would you hire for the following periods:

i two weeks?

ii four weeks?

iii twelve weeks?

Explain your answers.

b Use the graphs to complete the following difference tables:

i

TeleHire

w	c	Difference
0		
1		
2		
3		
4		

ii

TeleRent

w	c	Difference
0		
1		
2		
3		
4		

c For each company, use the difference tables in **b** to write:

    i   a formula for the cost (*c*) in terms of the number of weeks (*w*).

    ii an advertisement that includes the costs for renting.

10 A real-estate agent's weekly income (*y*) includes a retainer plus a percentage of the weekly sales. A *retainer* is a set fee for services from a client. The weekly sales (*x*) are expressed in sales units of $10 000.

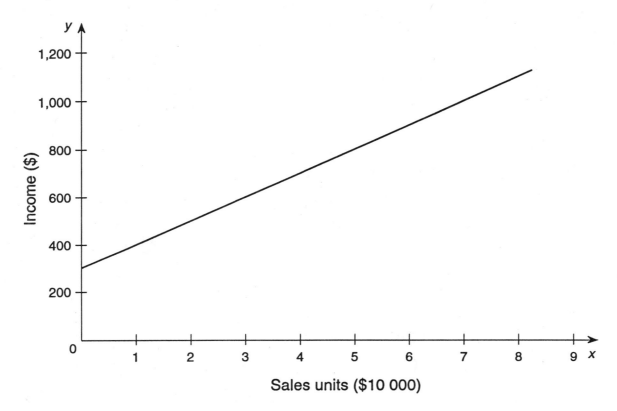

a Use the graph to complete the difference table.

x	y	Difference
0		
1		
2		
3		
4		

b **i** Write a formula for the agent's total weekly income.

    ii What income would the agent receive for a week in which the sales totaled $80000?

---

11 Mark wants to give candy to all his friends for Christmas. He finds this ad and decides to buys x pounds of candy for $\$y$.

**CHRISTMAS
Mail-Order
Special**

Candy $3.00 per pound
Shipping and Handling $4.00

x	y	Difference
0		
1	7	
2		
3		
4		

a i Complete the difference table for this problem.

   ii Write a formula for y (cost) in terms of x (pounds).

b Use your answer to **a ii** to write a formula for candy that costs $4.00 per pound, with a shipping and handling cost of $3.00.

c This graph shows $y = 3x + 4$, for $x \geq 0$.

   i Write the coordinates of points A, B, and C shown on the graph.

   ii Find the lengths of AB and BC.

   iii Find the quotient of AB ÷ BC.

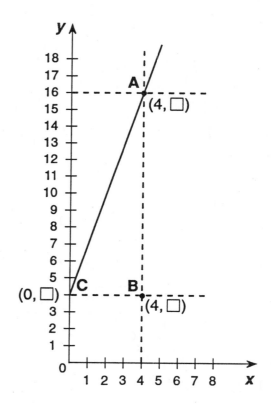

d Graph the formulas in the table below and look for patterns to help you complete the following table. (In each case, assume A and B are on the vertical line $x = 4$.)

Formula	Coordinates of Point C	AB ÷ BC
$y = 3x + 4$	(0, 4)	3
$y = 4x + 3$	(0, ☐)	☐
$y = 2x + 5$	(0, ☐)	☐

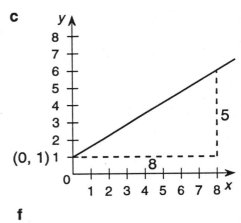

e AB ÷ BC is the *slope* of line AC. It shows the relationship between the *rise* (AB) of the line and the *run* (BC). In the general linear equation $y = ax + b$, what variable represents the line's slope?

f On your graph of $y = 2x + 5$, draw the line $x = 6$ and calculate its slope.

Is the value of AB ÷ BC the same as in the table in **d**? Explain your answer.

12 Use what you have learned in **11** to find the equation for each of the following graphs:

a

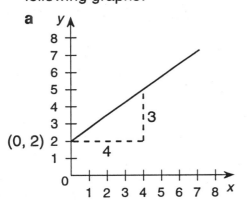

b

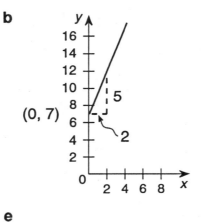

c

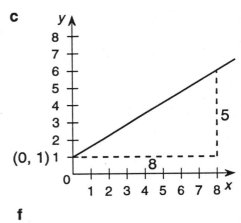

d

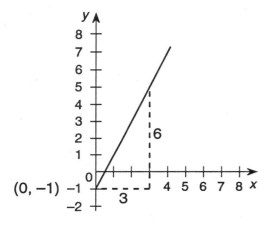

e

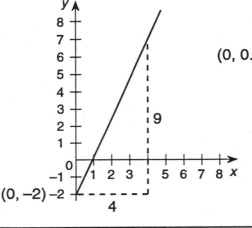

f

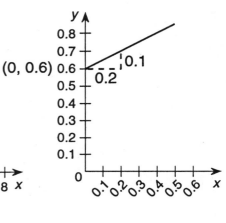

13 Black-and-white film takes y minutes to develop when the temperature of the developing chemical is $x°$ Celsius.

a Find a formula for y (number of minutes) in terms of x (temperature).

b What do you think happens to the accuracy of your formula when the temperature of the developing fluid reaches 54°C?

x (°C)	y (minutes)
16	27
18	24.5
20	22.0
22	19.5
24	17.0

14 Water freezes at 32°F (Fahrenheit) or 0°C (Celsius) and boils at 212°F or 100°C.

	Fahrenheit	Celsius
Water Freezes	32°	0°
Water Boils	212°	100°

Use what you have learned about interpreting graphs to find formulas for the following:

a Celsius in terms of Fahrenheit.

b Fahrenheit in terms of Celsius.

Hint: The slope of a line is constant. If you know the coordinates of just two points on the line you can find its slope. Try finding slope this way:

$$\frac{y_2 - y_1}{x_2 - x_1}$$

where (x_1, y_1) and (x_2, y_2) are any two points on the line.

Investigation Three

Discovering Quadratic Rules

1 This domino house has four stories and contaes 24 dominoes.

Jerry and Mandy try to beat the world record of 73 stories for a domino house. Before they begin, they want to know how many dominoes they'll need.

Mandy draws four simple domino houses. In each house there are *x* stories and *y* dominoes.

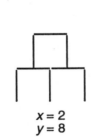

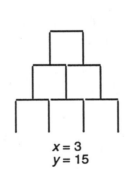

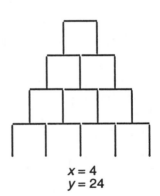

$x = 1$
$y = 3$

$x = 2$
$y = 8$

$x = 3$
$y = 15$

$x = 4$
$y = 24$

Jerry uses Mandy's diagrams to make this table.

a How many dominoes are needed for 7 stories?

b Jerry suggests that she continue the table for 8, 9, 10, ··· 74 stories. Is this a good strategy? Explain your answer.

x	y	First Difference
1	3	
		5
2	8	
		7
3	15	
		9
4	24	
		☐
5	35	
		☐
6	☐	
		☐
7	☐	

c Mandy suggests altering the table.

  i Complete Mandy's table and equation.

x	y	Pattern in y
1	3	1 × ☐
2	8	2 × ☐
3	15	3 × ☐
4	24	4 × ☐
5	☐	5 × ☐
⋮	⋮	⋮
74	☐	74 × ☐
x	y	x × ☐

$$y = x \times \square$$

  ii How many dominoes do Mandy and Jerry need for their record-breaking attempt?

d Show that the equation $y = x^2 + 2x$ is also correct.

MATHEMATICAL INVESTIGATIONS · DALE SEYMOUR PUBLICATIONS

2 Equations that involve relationships such as $y = x^2 + 2x$ are called *quadratic equations*. Jerry uses $y = x^2 + 2x$ and another quadratic equation, $y = 2x^2 - 3x + 1$, to make the following tables.

a i Complete each table.

  ii What do you notice about the second difference in each table?

x	y	First Difference	Second Difference
0	0		
		3	
1	3		□
		□	
2	8		□
		□	
3	15		□
		□	
4	24		□
		□	
5	□		

$y = x^2 + 2x$

x	y	First Difference	Second Difference
0	1		
		−1	
1	0		4
		3	
2	3		□
		□	
3	□		□
		□	
4	□		□
		□	
5	□		

$y = 2x^2 - 3x + 1$

b Prepare difference tables similar to Jerry's for each of the following quadratic equations:

  i $y = x^2 + 6x - 1$

  ii $y = 4x^2 - 8x + 9$

  iii $y = 2x^2 + x + 4$

  iv $y = -x^2 + 6x + 8$

> **What rule do your tables suggest about second differences for quadratic equations?**

c To confirm the rule from **b**, Jerry makes a table for the general quadratic equation: $y = ax^2 + bx + c$.

i Complete this table.

x	y	First Difference	Second Difference
0	c		
		a + b	
1	a + b + c		2a
		3a + b	
2	4a + 2b + c		_____
		_____	
3	_____		_____
		_____	
4	_____		

ii Does the table confirm your rule? Explain your answer.

3 Mandy now sees how to use second-difference tables to find quadratic rules. She uses her domino-house results and Jerry's table from **2 c**.

$$y = x^2 + 2x \text{ (Dominoes)}$$

x	y	First Difference	Second Difference
0	0		
		3	
1	3		2
		5	
2	8		2
		7	
3	15		2
		9	
4	24		

$$y = ax^2 + bx + c$$

x	y	First Difference	Second Difference
0	c		
		a + b	
1	a + b + c		2a
		3a + b	
2	4a + 2b + c		2a
		5a + b	
3	9a + 3b + c		2a
		7a + b	
4	16a + 4b + c		

a Compare the shaded parts in the two tables to help you explain why:

i $c = 0$

ii $a = 1$, and therefore $b = 2$.

b Do the equations in **a** confirm that $y = x^2 + 2x$? Explain your answer.

c Use Mandy's method to find a formula for this table.

x	y	First Difference	Second Difference
0	3		
		5	
1	8		2
		7	
2	15		2
		9	
3	24		2
		11	
4	35		

4 Find a formula that relates *x* and *y* for each of the following tables:

a

x	y
0	1
1	4
2	9
3	16
4	25

b

x	y
0	1
1	3
2	9
3	19
4	33

c

x	y
0	1
1	3
2	11
3	25
4	45

d

x	y
0	☐
1	5
2	16
3	33
4	56

e

x	y
0	☐
1	1
2	3
3	6
4	10

f

x	y
0	☐
1	24
2	50
3	88
4	138

5 This diagram shows a three-story "house of cards."

a Find a formula for the number of cards (*y*) for a house of cards with *x* stories.

b How many cards are needed for 100 stories?

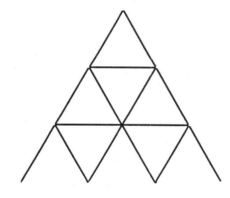

6 At a school graduation ceremony, every graduate congratulates every other graduate by shaking hands.

Altogether there are 274 graduates.

a Find a formula for the number of handshakes (*y*) for *x* graduates.

b What is the total number of handshakes among graduates at the graduation ceremony?

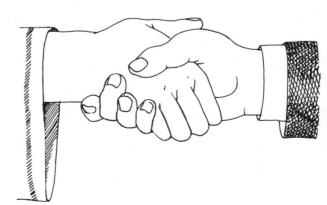

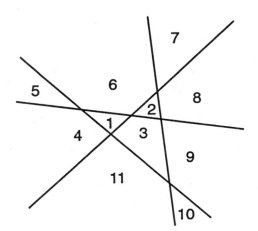

7 Ed draws *x* straight lines so that each line intersects every other line.

No three lines pass through the same point. This creates *y* regions (*x* = 4 intersecting lines, so *y* = 11 regions).

a Use a difference table to find a formula that gives the number of regions (*y*) using *x* lines.

b How many regions can be made from 100 intersecting lines?

8 In this table, *y* is the sum of the first *x* even numbers.

x	*y*	First Difference	Second Difference
0	☐		
1	2		
2	6		
3	12		
4	☐		
5	☐		

a Use the table to find a formula for *y* in terms of *x*.

b Find the sum of the first 1,000 even numbers.

c Find a formula for the sum of the first *x* odd numbers.

d Find a formula for the sum of the first *x* whole numbers.

e Find formulas for the sum of the first *x* numbers in each of the following series:

i $2 + 5 + 8 + 11 + \cdots$

ii $1 + 5 + 9 + 13 + \cdots$

iii $0.6 + 0.8 + 1.0 + 1.2 + \cdots$

iv $100 + 97 + 94 + 91 + \cdots$

v $48 + 47 + 46 + 45 + \cdots$

vi $a + (a + d) + (a + 2d) + (a + 3d) + \cdots$

9 The pentagonal numbers are shown in the following figure:

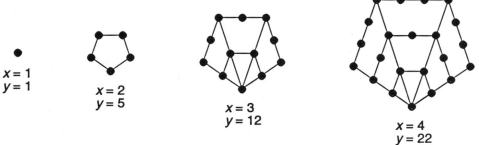

$x = 1$
$y = 1$

$x = 2$
$y = 5$

$x = 3$
$y = 12$

$x = 4$
$y = 22$

For example, the 4th pentagonal number is 22.

a Find a formula that allows you to predict the xth pentagonal number (y).

b What is the 100th pentagonal number?

10 The hexagonal numbers are shown in the following figure:

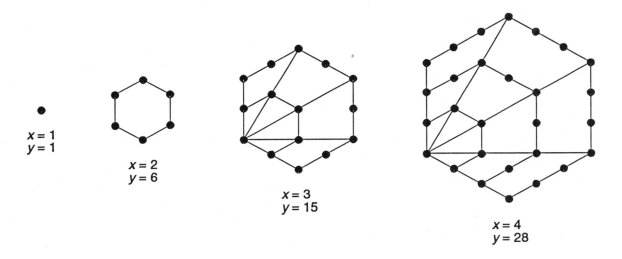

$x = 1$
$y = 1$

$x = 2$
$y = 6$

$x = 3$
$y = 15$

$x = 4$
$y = 28$

For example, the 4th hexagonal number is 28.

a Find a formula that allows you to predict the xth hexagonal number (y).

b What is the 100th hexagonal number?

MATHEMATICAL INVESTIGATIONS • DALE SEYMOUR PUBLICATIONS

11 A cube of side x is constructed from unit cubes. The surface of the cube is painted so that y unit cubes have paint on one or more of their faces.

$x = 2$
$y = 8$

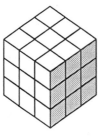

$x = 3$
$y = 26$

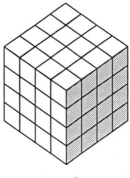

$x = 4$
$y = 56$

Frank looks at a $5 \times 5 \times 5$ cube and realizes it contains a $3 \times 3 \times 3$ cube inside it. None of the unit cubes that make up the $3 \times 3 \times 3$ cube is painted, but all the other unit cubes are.

a If $x = 5$, show that $y = 98$.

b Use Frank's method to find y for the following values of x:

  i $x = 6$

  ii $x = 7$

  iii $x = 8$

  iv $x = 12$

c Use the geometric shapes and Frank's method to explain why:
$$y = x^3 - (x - 2)^3.$$

d Prepare a difference table and find a quadratic formula for y in terms of x.

x	y	First Difference	Second Difference
0	☐		
1	☐		
2	8		
3	26		
4	56		
5	98		
6	☐		

e Can you now show that $x^3 - (x-2)^3 = 6x^2 - 12x + 8$?

㉙ Why is this true?

f Let z equal the number of unit cubes with three faces painted.

㉚ Let u equal the number of unit cubes with two faces painted.

Let w equal the number of unit cubes with one face painted.

Construct a difference table to find a formula for:

i z in terms of x.

ii u in terms of x.

iii w in terms of x.

g Add the three formulas in **f** to show that $y = z + u + w$.

ON YOUR OWN

Four green frogs sit on lily pads and four brown frogs sit on their own lily pads. There is one spare pad between them. No pad can support more than one frog on it at a time.

The green frogs are going to change places with the brown frogs. The frogs can either:

a hop to an adjacent unused pad.

b jump over another frog to an unused pad.

1 Find the *minimum* number of moves (either hops or jumps) required for the frog interchange. Hint: Do not allow frogs to go backwards.

2 If there are *n* frogs of each color, find a formula in terms of *n* for the *minimum* number of moves.

3 For *n* frogs of each color, show how many hops to an adjacent pad and jumps over another frog are necessary. How does this relate to your general formula for moves?

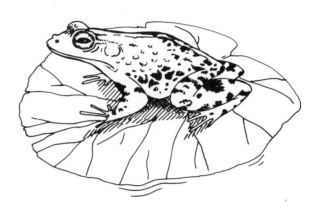

Investigation Four

Exploring More Complex Rules

1 At Joe's fruit stand, oranges are stacked in the shape of a square-based pyramid.

Joe needs a formula to help make decisions about stacking fruit. He wants to know:

- how many oranges should be arranged in the bottom layer (the xth layer from the top).
- how many oranges (y) can be stacked in a pyramid with x layers.

He counts the oranges in the top layer, the top two layers, the top three layers, and the top four layers—then records his results in a table.

$x = 1$

$x = 2$

$x = 3$

$x = 4$

a Use Joe's table to find the number of oranges in:

i the 10th layer.

ii an entire pyramid with 10 layers.

x	y
1	1 = 1
2	1+4 = 5
3	1 + 4 + 9 = 14
4	1 + 4 + 9 + 16 = 30
5	
6	
7	
8	
9	
10	

b To find a formula for y in terms of x, Joe makes a difference table. Note that he also includes an imaginary value for y when $x = 0$ (the 0th layer).

x	y	First Difference	Second Difference	Third Difference
0	☐			
		☐		
1	1		☐	
		4		☐
2	5		5	
		9		☐
3	14		7	
		16		☐
4	30		☐	
		☐		
5	☐			

i Complete Joe's table.

ii After carefully evaluating the completed difference table, Joe concludes that the relationship is not a quadratic but a third-degree equation. This is also called a *cubic equation*. Explain his reasoning. Hint: The general form for a cubic equation is: $y = ax^3 + bx^2 + cx + d$.

iii Complete the following difference table for the general cubic equation: $y = ax^3 + bx^2 + cx + d$.

x	y	First Difference	Second Difference	Third Difference
0	d			
		$a + b + c$		
1	$a + b + c + d$		$6a + 2b$	
		$7a + 3b + c$		$6a$
2	$8a + 4b + 2c + d$		$12a + 2b$	
		$19a + 5b + c$		
3	$27a + 9b + 3c + d$			
4				
5				

iv Use the entries in Joe's and the general cubic difference table to help you find a, b, c, and d. Write an equation that can predict the number of oranges (y) for a square pyramid with x layers.

v Joe finds the following formula in a college textbook:

$$1^2 + 2^2 + \cdots\cdots + n^2 = \frac{1}{6}\, n\,(n + 1)(2n + 1)$$

Does this formula also give the total number of oranges in a square pyramid with n layers?

2 Sue challenges Anna to find the total number of squares on an 8×8 chessboard. Anna begins by counting all the possible squares on some simpler boards: 1×1, 2×2, 3×3, and so on. The following table shows her results.

Size of Board	1×1 Squares	2×2 Squares	3×3 Squares	4×4 Squares	Total Squares
1×1	1	—	—	—	1
2×2	4	1	—	—	5
3×3	9	4	1	—	14
4×4	16	9	4	1	30

a Use patterns you find in the table to help solve Anna's problem for an 8×8 chessboard. Try constructing a difference table to come up with an equation.

b Find a formula for the total number of squares on an $n \times n$ chessboard.

3 Joe stacks apples in the shape of rectangular pyramids with one more apple in the length than the width. This diagram shows the top three layers of the pyramid.

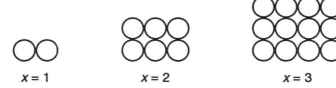

$x = 1$ $\qquad$ $x = 2$ $\qquad$ $x = 3$

Find a formula for the number of apples (y) in a rectangular pyramid with x layers.

On YOUR OWN

This 2×2 square grid contains a total of 9 rectangles.

Find a formula for the number of rectangles in an $n \times n$ grid.

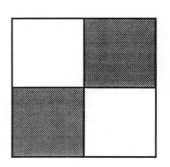

4 Sue works at a grocery store. She stacks cans of beans in triangular pyramids.

This diagram shows the top three layers.

$x = 1$ $x = 2$ $x = 3$

Find a formula for the number of cans (y) in a pyramid with x layers.

5 Construct a difference table and find a formula for each of the following:

a

x	y
0	0
1	2
2	10
3	30
4	68

b

x	y
0	0
1	1
2	14
3	51
4	124

c

x	y
0	0
1	3
2	14
3	39
4	84

d

x	y
0	□
1	2
2	4
3	0
4	−16
5	−50

e

x	y
0	□
1	4
2	12
3	18
4	16
5	0

f

x	y
0	□
1	8
2	12
3	26
4	56
5	108

6 a Fourth-degree equations are called *quartic equations* and come in the form $y = ax^4 + bx^3 + cx^2 + dx + e$. This is the difference table for the general equation:

x	y	First Difference	Second Difference	Third Difference	Fourth Difference
0	e				
		$a+b+c+d$			
1	$a+b+c+d+e$		$14a+6b+2c$		
		$15a+7b+3c+d$		$36a+6b$	
2	$16a+8b+4c+2d+e$		$50a+12b+2c$		$24a$
		$65a+19b+5c+d$		$60a+6b$	
3	$81a+27b+9c+3d+e$		$110a+18b+2c$		$24a$
		$175a+37b+7c+d$		$84a+6b$	
4	$256a+64b+16c+4d+e$		$194a+24b+2c$		$24a$
		$369a+61b+9c+d$		$108a+6b$	
5	$625a+125b+25c+5d+e$		$302a+30b+2c$		
		$671a+91b+11c+d$			
6	$1296a+216b+36c+6d+e$				

Find a *quartic* formula for y in terms of n where
$$y = 1^3 + 2^3 + 3^3 + \cdots\cdots + n^3$$

b Find formulas for the following:

i $y = (1 \times 2) + (2 \times 3) + (3 \times 4) + \cdots + n(n+1)$

ii $y = (0 \times 1) + (1 \times 2) + (2 \times 3) + \cdots + (n-1)n$

iii $y = (1^2 \times 2) + (2^2 \times 3) + (3^2 \times 4) + \cdots + n^2(n+1)$

7 Each of the five points on the circumference of this circle is connected to every other point on the circle. The circle is divided into sixteen regions.

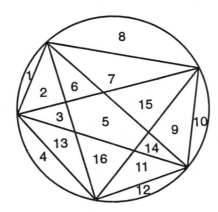

a What is the greatest number of regions possible when six points are connected? (The answer is *not* 32!)

b Find a formula connecting the number of regions *(y)* to the number of points *(x)*.

CHECK-UP

1 A child uses y matchsticks to make x houses as shown below.

$x = 1$
$y = 7$

$x = 2$
$y = 13$

$x = 3$
$y = \boxed{}$

a Find a formula for y in terms of x. Justify your answer using geometric patterns you find in the figures.

b If $x = 80$, find the value of y.

2 Newtown has a bus station at the intersection of 1st Street and 1st Avenue. A visitor to Newtown can get a taxi at the bus station.

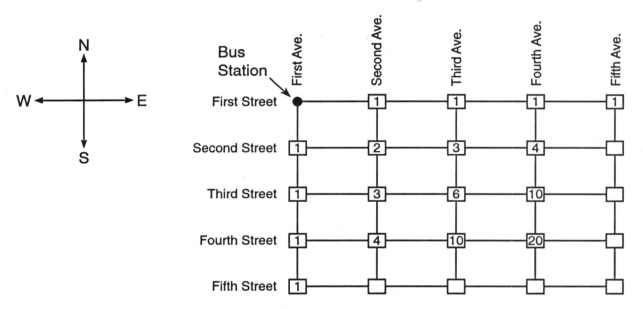

a Complete the pattern of numbers in the empty boxes.

b The numbers in the boxes show the number of *different* ways a taxi can reach an intersection by traveling only east and south. (Remember: The taxi always starts at the bus station.) Find formulas for the number of ways of reaching the following intersections:

   i   1st Avenue and nth Street.   **iv**   4th Avenue and nth Street.

   ii 2nd Avenue and nth Street.   **v** nth Avenue and 4th Street.

   iii 3rd Avenue and nth Street.

CHAPTER FOUR

EXPLORING RATES

TEACHING NOTES

Rates are ratios between two types of quantities—such as distance and time or money and time. Many everyday events are described in terms of rates to aid communication about complex relationships—for example, the speed of a moving object or interest rates in finance. Uniform and changing rates, instantaneous speed, and maxima and minima problems are introduced in this chapter. Please note: Since many investigations in this chapter rely on finding equations that represent data in tables, students should first complete the finite-difference activities in Chapter Three.

Investigation One • Uniform Rates

Examples of uniform rates are the speed of a train moving at a constant pace and a fixed-mortgage rate that does not vary over the life of the loan. A uniform rate can be represented by the slope of a straight-line graph of a linear equation (that is, change in *y* divided by the change in *x*). Since the slope of the line remains constant for any point on the line, the rate of change is uniform. This section includes investigations into weaving carpets, calculating fuel costs, measuring electricity, and determining speed that demonstrate the use of uniform rates in everyday situations.

Investigation Two • Changing Rates

An example of changing rates is the speed of an arrow shot into the air. Starting with the initial velocity of the arrow as it leaves the bow, the arrow gradually slows until it reaches its highest point (when its vertical speed equals zero) and then increases velocity until it strikes the ground at nearly the same speed as when it left the bow. A variable-rate mortgage adjusts the interest charged according to some base rate such as the Prime Rate or twelve-month T-bill Rate. Of course, this type of variable rate is generally not as continuous or predictable as the rate of a falling object.

The concept of *average speed* is introduced as an aid to understanding changing rates. For example, if a parachutist falls 5 meters in the first second, she falls at an average rate of $\frac{5-0}{1} = 5$ meters per second during the entire first second. If she falls a total of 20 meters by the end of the next second, her average speed during that second only is $\frac{20-5}{1} = 15$ meters per second. However, the average rate of descent for the first two seconds is $\frac{20-0}{2} = 10$ meters per second. In this section, students calculate the speed of a parachutist, the area of a flood, the spread of an inkblot, the speed of a baseball hit straight up into the air, balls rolling down a hill, and a wrench dropped from a spacecraft to the moon. Students look for patterns in tables and find the quadratic equations that represent distance traveled in terms of time.

Investigation Three • Instantaneous Rates

Instantaneous speeds for objects traveling at continuously changing rates (for example, a falling rock) can be determined using the techniques found in calculus. Speed at a given instant can be approximated by finding the speed over a very short time span (such as 0.0001 seconds). Creating a table of speeds over shorter and shorter time intervals and focusing on the converging pattern helps students to conceptualize the notion of the limit as a specific instant in time is approached.

Students first use this technique to approximate the instantaneous speed of an accelerating car at specific times. They then look for patterns in time, distance, and speed tables to find the relationship between pairs of distance and speed formulas, both of which are written as a function of time. For example, for d = distance, t = time, and s = speed, if $d = t^2$, then $s = 2t$; if $d = 3t^2$, then $s = 2 \times 3t = 6t$; and so on. Note that the relationship between the distance and speed formulas is, in fact, the *derivative* operation in calculus. In this section, students calculate the instantaneous speeds of accelerating and braking cars, falling objects, fruit-fly populations, a raft shooting the rapids, and the price of stocks.

Investigation Four • Maxima and Minima

Using the speed formula associated with a given distance formula helps when exploring the maximum and minimum points on the trajectory of an object or graph of a function. All the examples in this section involve a quadratic distance formula, since many natural motions and phenomena are governed by such equations. For example, suppose the height of an arrow shot straight up into the air can be calculated using the formula $h = 30t - 5t^2$. We can find how long it takes the arrow to reach the highest point by constructing a table showing the height at one-second intervals. However, by using the associated speed formula $s = 30 - 10t$, we can set the speed s to zero (the arrow has zero speed at the highest point) and solve the equation for t ($0 = 30 - 10t$, so $t = 3$ seconds). The height of the arrow at the highest point can be computed by substituting 3 in the height formula: $h = (30 \times 3) - (5 \times 9)$; so $h = 45$ meters. In this investigation, students explore maxima and minima problems associated with dropping a yo-yo, designing a floor plan, enclosing a field with a fence, and pricing airline tickets. Each problem is more easily solved by working with the speed formula associated with each given distance (area or cost) formula. These exercises provide a conceptual introduction to the derivative, one of the basic ideas in elementary calculus, by encouraging the inductive application of prior knowledge of patterns, functions, and finite differences.

Investigation One

Uniform Rates

1   A three-meter-wide automatic loom is used to weave floor carpet.
    Suppose it weaves *d* millimeters of carpet in *t* seconds. The table
    shows the total length of the carpet after zero seconds, one second,
    two seconds, and so on.

t (s)	*d* (mm)	Pattern
0	0	☐ × 0
1	12	☐ × 1
2	24	☐ × 2
3	36	☐ × 3
4		☐ × 4
t		☐ × *t*

$$d = \boxed{} \times t$$

   What length of carpet is made in:

   i   the first second only?

   ii   the second second only?

   iii the third second only?

b   Is the loom working at a uniform (constant) rate? If so, what is this
        rate?

c   Complete the table and equation that summarizes the pattern.

d   Describe how the equation in **c** is related to the rate in **b**.

e   For each formula below, write the speed or *rate* (in millimeters/
        second) at which carpet is being produced.

   i $d = 13t$

   ii $d = 8.7t$

   iii $d = 18.4t$

2 The cost (*p* dollars) of *w* pounds of tomatoes is given in the table.

| QUALITY $ ☐/lb. |
| TOMATOES |

a Fill in the supermarket price label.

b Complete the formula: $p = \square\, w$

How is this formula related to the selling rate for tomatoes?

w	p
2	5.00
3	7.50
4	10.00
7	17.50

3 An engine drives a concrete mixer in a remote area. It uses *p* gallons of gasoline in *t* hours.

a Find the rate of gasoline consumption in gallons/hour.

t (h)	p (g)	Pattern
0	0	☐ × 0
2	1	☐ × 2
4	2	☐ × 4
6	3	
8	4	
t		☐ × t

$$p = \square\, t$$

b Why is it reasonable to expect a uniform consumption rate for this engine?

c i Complete the table and equation.

ii How is this equation related to the rate of consumption?

iii Make a graph of the *t* and *p* coordinates in the table. Is the equation in **ii** a linear equation? Explain your answer.

d Complete the table for several engines that consume gasoline uniformly. Each line in the table represents a different engine.

Engine	t (h)	p (g)	Formula
1	6	3	$p = 0.5t$
2	8	6	$p = \square t$
3	10	7	$p = \square t$
4	20	19	$p = \square t$
5	100	63	$p = \square t$
6	3		$p = 2t$
7	4		$p = 0.6t$
8	10		$p = 1.8t$
9		9	$p = 1.8t$
10		20	$p = 4t$

4 The *joule* is the basic unit of energy used to measure amounts of electricity. If an electrical device uses one joule of electricity per second, the device has an electrical rating of 1 *watt*. Light bulbs are often rated at 25 watts, 40 watts, or 100 watts. One-thousand watts is called 1 kilowatt (kw).

Suppose an electric coffee maker is turned on for two minutes and uses a total of 240,000 joules of electrical energy.

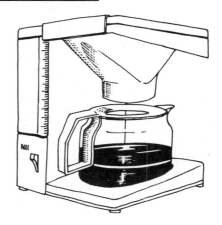

a Show that the coffee maker uses energy at a rate of 2,000 joules per second.

b Explain why the rating for this coffee maker is 2 kilowatts.

c If *E* kilojoules (1 kilojoule = 1,000 joules) of energy is used in *t* seconds, complete the equation for the coffee maker: $E = \square t$.

d Write down the rating (in kilowatts) for electric heaters with the following energy equations.

   i $E = 3.1t$

   ii $E = 0.9t$

   iii $E = 2.6t$

       MATHEMATICAL INVESTIGATIONS • DALE SEYMOUR PUBLICATIONS

ON YOUR OWN

1   Find out the ratings of the appliances used in your home and how long your family uses them each day. Also look at a recent electricity bill and determine what your family pays per kilowatt hour. Note that in some areas electricity costs increase if you use more than an allotted "lifeline" amount each month.

2   Calculate the costs of running your appliances. Think of ways to reduce your electricity bill that will not leave your family cold and hungry.

5   It takes *t* hours for an experienced jogger to run *d* kilometers at a constant speed. His speed is 15 kilometers per hour.

a   Complete the equation $d = \square t$, which relates distance and time for this runner.

b   Complete the following table in which each line represents a different runner. (Speed is in kilometers per hour.)

Runner	Speed (*s*) (km/h)	Formula
1	15	
2	17	
3	8	
4	11	
5		$d = 7.3t$
6		$d = 14.8t$
7		$d = 11.5t$
8		$d = 5t$

6 M.Y. Martin and Company offers a special deal. A school pays a total of $C to buy x calculators.

> ## M. Y. Martin and Co.
> ## Special Deal
> ---
> ## Scientific Calculators
> **$21.49 per calculator**
> **Only $3.00 postage**
> for any order—regardless of how many calculators!

a Complete this formula that represents the cost of M. Y. Martin calculators: $C = \Box x + \triangle$

b i Various firms offer similar deals to M.Y. Martin for the same calculator. Complete this table.

Firm	Equation	Cost of Calculator ($)	Postage ($)
M.Y. Martin	$C = 21.49x + \triangle$		3.00
Cheapsales, Inc.	$C = 19.99x + 7.30$		
Brown & Brown	$C = \Box x + 3.80$	20.25	
Ron Ripper, Inc.	$C = 24.49x + 6.30$		
Discounters, Inc.	$C = \Box x + \triangle$	21.00	3.50

ii If your school wants 12 calculators, who should the school buy from? Why?

iii If your school has $700 to spend on calculators, which firm should the school buy from? Why?

c A radio costs $84 now. The manufacturer expects the price to rise by $6 per year. If the cost is $C, write a formula for C in n years time.

7 A train traveling at 20 meters/second enters a tunnel. The train's porter starts her stopwatch just as the front of the train enters. Suppose the front of the train has gone d meters into the tunnel after t seconds.

7

a Complete the equation: $d_{front} = \boxed{}t$

b If the train is 60 meters long, complete the equation for d (the distance into the tunnel for the *end* of the train): $d_{end} = 20t - \boxed{}$.

c The equation for the porter's position on the train is $d = 20t - 35$. How far is she from the front of the train?

d If the tunnel is 800 meters long, how long does it take for the entire train to complete the journey through the tunnel?

e The porter repeats her experiment when she is on another train. Her equation for the *end* of this train is $d_{porter} = 16t - 80$.

   i How long is the train?

   ii How fast is the train going?

f How long does it take for the entire train in **e** to complete the journey through the tunnel?

8 In a *handicap* race, the fastest runner begins the race at the starting line. Slower runners are each given the advantage of starting an appropriate distance along the track. The idea is to position each runner so that the race will end in a tie—assuming each competitor runs at a uniform speed.

Therefore, for a handicap race where d is the distance of a runner from the starting line after t seconds, $d = \boxed{}t + \triangle$. ($\boxed{}$ = individual running speed in meters/second and $\triangle$ = handicap distance in meters.)

a Complete the table for the different runners.

Name	Equation	Speed (m/s)	Handicap (m)
Marilyn	$d = 8t + 12$	8	12.0
Lesley	$d = 7.5t + \triangle$		15.2
Anna	$d = 8.6t + \triangle$		5.2
Hannah	$d = \square t + 14$	7.3	
Ruth	$d = \square t + \triangle$	8.1	5.6
Crystal	$d = \square t + 0$	9.0	

b Do you think these handicaps will make a fair 100-meter race?

9 In a mixed men's and women's sprint, Karl can run 10 meters/second and Cindy 9 meters/second. Murray, the handicapper, tries to start the runners at different distances along the 180-meter track so that the race will be a tie. Karl begins at the starting line.

a How long does Karl take to run the race?

b How far does Cindy run in Karl's time for **a**?

c Where should Cindy start so that the race will be fair?

d Sally begins at the starting line in a 100-meter race. Find the handicaps for Joanne, Mary, and Jules if they race with Sally.

e Jules and Mary compete in a 200-meter race. Find Jules' handicap.

f Do you think this process of handicapping will work in a real race?

Karl	10 m/s
Cindy	9 m/s
Sally	10 m/s
Joanne	9 m/s
Mary	8 m/s
Jules	7 m/s

10 In a marathon, Rosa runs 15 feet/second. She runs d meters in t seconds.

a Complete Rosa's distance equation: $d = \square t$

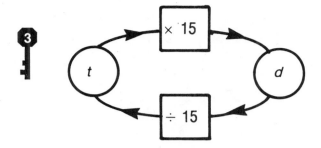

MARATHON

26.219 miles —>

b i Find how long it takes for her to run
1 foot. (Don't round yet.)

ii Show why Rosa takes about 5.87 minutes or 5 minutes and 52
seconds to run 1 mile. Why do you need the answer for **b i** to
find this result?

c How long will Rosa take to run a marathon if she runs a constant 15
feet/second?

d i Complete this table. (Round only the last column to the nearest
second.)

Runner	Constant Speed (ft/s) (1)	Time for 1 foot (s) (2)	Time for 1 mile (s)	Time for 1 mile (min and s)
Rosa	15			
Leanne	14			
Randy	11			
Murray	12			
Peter	10			
Kevin	16			

ii For each row in the table, multiply the number in column (1) with
the number in column (2). Is there a pattern in the products?

e Use the reciprocal key ($\frac{1}{x}$) on your calculator to complete these

tables. (Round sensibly.)

i

Speed (ft/s)	Rate (s/ft)
4.3	
11.6	
0.962	
5.814	

ii

Speed (ft/s)	Rate (s/ft)
	0.0491
	0.063
	1.338
	0.7192

11 The table shows the distance (*d* feet) a car has traveled in *t* seconds after leaving a stoplight.

t	d
0	0
1	3
2	12
3	27
4	48
5	75
6	105
7	135
8	165

a Use the finite-differences method to determine if the car traveled at a constant speed.

b i If $t \geq 5$ seconds, what is the speed of the car in feet per second? In miles per hour?

ii If $t \geq 5$ seconds, find a formula for *d*.

iii If $t \leq 5$ seconds, find a formula for *d*.

iv Graph the *t* and *d* coordinates in the table. What happens to the line? Why? (Hint: You will need a large sheet of graph paper to accommodate the *d*-axis.)

ON YOUR OWN

A marathon runner plans to run a marathon of 26.219 miles in 2 hours and 14 minutes.

1 What rate (minutes/mile) should he plan for? Why do runners use minutes/mile instead of the more common speed rating of mile/minute or miles/hour when planning their race times?

2 Ideally he should maintain this rate throughout the race. In practice he splits the race into different rates. Explain why he has to do this.

3 In a cycling race, constant speeds are not maintained throughout the race. Find out why.

4 Do swimmers move at a constant rate or plan split times?

Investigation Two

Changing Rates

When an object falls, it speeds up—or *accelerates.* That means its speed changes as time goes by. In this investigation, the *average speed* of a moving object is the distance it travels during a given time interval.

1 A parachutist drops *d* feet in *t* seconds during free fall from a small airplane.

t	d
0	0
1	16
2	64
3	144
4	256

a Find the average speed during

 i the first second.

   ii the second second.

   iii the third second.

   iv the fourth second.

b Predict the average speed during the fifth second.

c Remember that $s = \dfrac{d}{t}$. So, is the average speed during the sixth second

   i <, >, or = the speed at exactly 5 seconds?

   ii <, >, or = the speed at exactly 6 seconds?

d i Construct a table of the time intervals (0, 1, 2, 3, . . .) and the average speed for each interval ($t = 0$–1 is the first interval). Use the finite-differences method to construct a formula that predicts the parachutist's average speed for each interval in feet/seconds. Then calculate the average speed during the twentieth second in feet/seconds and in miles/hour.

ii Think about the speed of falling raindrops and decide whether the answer in **d i** is unrealistic. Explain why.

e This graph shows how the speed of an object changes during free fall.

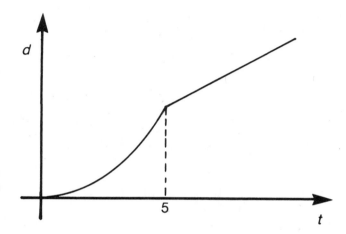

i What happens to the rate of fall after about 5 seconds?

ii Explain *terminal velocity*.

2 After t hours of flooding, x acres of land near the river mouth are covered by floodwaters.

$$x = \square\, t^{\square}$$

a Use the finite-differences method to discover the equation that relates time and the area of flooding.

b Show that the rate of flooding in the third hour averages 15 acres per hour.

c Show that between $t = 2$ and $t = 4$ the average rate of flooding is 18 acres/hour.

d Find the average rate of flooding in the sixth hour.

e Why is it unrealistic to use the flooding equation in **a** for all values of t ?

t	x
0	0
1	3
2	12
3	27
4	48
5	
6	

3 The table shows the area (A mm^2) of an inkblot as it increases in time (t seconds).

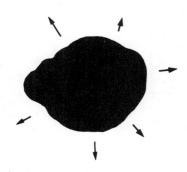

t	A
0	0
1	2
2	8
3	18
4	32

$$A = \square\, t^{\square}$$

a Use the finite-differences method to find the equation that relates time and the area of the blot.

b What will the area be after

  i 10 seconds?

  ii 11 seconds?

  iii What is the *average* rate of increase in the eleventh second?

c Should you use the equation in **a** to find the average rate of area increase after 30 seconds? Explain your answer.

4 Sebastian makes P dollars of profit in his business during the nth year of operation.

a Complete the table and use the finite-differences method to find the equation that relates time and profit.

b At what rate does Sebastian's profit grow during the

  i third year?

  ii sixth year?

n	P
1	100
2	800
3	2,700
4	6,400
5	
6	

$$P = \square\, n^{\square}$$

5 Find formulas for each set of data.

a

t	d
0	0
1	4
2	16
3	36
4	64

$d = \square\,t^{\square}$

b

x	y
0	0
1	0.5
2	2
3	4.5
4	8

$y = \square\,x^{\square}$

c

x	V
0	0
1	2
2	16
3	54
4	128

$V = \square\,x^{\square}$

d

x	T
0	0
1	4
2	32
3	108
4	256

$T = \square\,x^{\square}$

6 A baseball is popped straight up above the batter. The ball is *h* meters above the ground after *t* seconds.

t	h
0.0	0.00
0.5	8.75
1.0	15.00
1.5	18.75
2.0	20.00
2.5	18.75
3.0	15.00
3.5	8.75
4.0	0.00

a Show that the average speed between times $t = 0.5$ second and $t = 1$ second is 12.5 meters/second.

b Complete the table by calculating the average speed for each time interval.

Time Interval (seconds)	Distance Traveled (meters)	Average Speed (m/s)
0.0–0.5	$8.75 - 0.0 = 8.75$	
0.5–1.0	$15 - 8.75 = 6.25$	12.5
1.0–1.5		
1.5–2.0		
2.0–2.5	$18.75 - 20 = {}^-1.25$	$^-2.5$
2.5–3.0		
3.0–3.5		
3.5–4.0		

c Explain what a *negative* average speed in **b** means.

d Find a formula that relates time t and distance h for the baseball. Hint: To use the finite-differences method, t values must be at intervals of one second: 0, 1, 2, 3, and so on.

e Data for another ball is shown in the table. Is the ball speeding up or slowing down? Explain your answer.

t	h
0	0
0.2	1.8
0.4	3.2
0.6	4.2
0.8	4.8
1.0	5.0

7 Galileo, the Italian astronomer and physicist, discovered laws of motion for rolling a ball down a slope. In this example, the ball rolls d meters in t seconds.

a Is the ball speeding up or slowing down? Explain your answer.

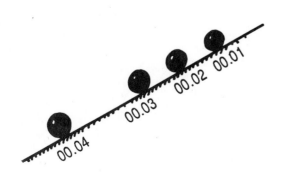

b Suppose a car drives down the slope at a constant rate of 8 meters/second. A physicist at the side of the road releases a ball so that it starts rolling alongside the car at $t = 0$. Complete the following table.

Time (t) (seconds)	Ball (d) (meters)	Car's Distance (meters)
0	0	0
1	2	8
2	8	16
3	18	
4		
5		

c Is the ball or the car ahead after

i 1 second?

ii 2 seconds?

iii 3 seconds?

iv 4 seconds?

v 5 seconds?

d From 0 to 4 seconds, the average speed of the ball is the same as the constant speed of the car. Explain why.

8 A wrench falls out of an Apollo spacecraft and drops d meters in t seconds to the moon's surface.

a Is the wrench speeding up as it falls?

b **i** How far does the wrench fall between $t = 2$ and $t = 5$?

ii How long does it take to drop the distance in **i** ?

iii Find the average speed for this time interval (from $t = 2$ to $t = 5$).

t (seconds)	d (meters)
0	0
1	1
2	4
3	9
4	16
5	25

c Complete the following table.

Time at Start t_1 (seconds)	Distance from Start d_1 (meters)	Time at End t_2 (seconds)	Distance from Start d_2 (meters)	Average Speed in the Interval (meters/second)
2	4	5	25	$\dfrac{25 - 4}{5 - 2} = 7$
2		3		
3		4		
4		5		
0		3		
t_1	d_1	t_2	d_2	$\dfrac{\square - \square}{\square - \square}$

d Write the formula for calculating the average speed of the falling wrench during an interval of time.

9 A river levee starts to give way, letting water flow into the surrounding fields. The total volume of water that flows through the break in t seconds is w cubic meters (m³).

t	w
0	0
1	5
2	20
3	45
4	80
5	125

a Is the break in the levee getting worse?

b **i** How much water escapes between $t = 2$ and $t = 5$?

  ii What is the average rate of water loss (in m^3/s) between $t = 2$ and $t = 5$?

c Complete the following table by calculating the average rate of water loss for the specified periods of time. Write a general formula by using the example in the last row to calculate the average rate of water loss.

Time at Start t_1 (seconds)	Water Escaped by Start w_1 (m^3)	Time at End t_2 (seconds)	Water Escaped by End w_2 (m^3)	Average Rate of Water Loss (m^3/seconds)
0	0	1	5	$\dfrac{5 - 0}{1 - 0} = 5$
1	5	2	20	
2		3		
3		4		
4		5		
2	20	5	125	$\dfrac{125 - 20}{5 - 2} = 35$
0		5		
t_1	w_1	t_2	w_2	$\dfrac{\square - \square}{\square - \square}$

d **i** Use the finite-differences method on the original table of t and w values to discover a formula that relates time in seconds (t) and the volume of water loss (w).

  ii Use this formula to predict how long it will take for 50,000 m^3 of water to flow through the hole in the levee.

Investigation Three

Instantaneous Rates

In the first two investigations, you have calculated the average speed of an object for a given time interval by using the $s = d \div t$ formula. In this investigation, you'll use average speeds in another way to calculate the exact speed of a moving object—especially an object that moves at continuously changing rates. This is called calculating *instantaneous speed.*

1   A Porsche stops at an intersection, then moves toward a highway patrol officer with a radar gun. The car travels *d* feet from the intersection in *t* seconds.

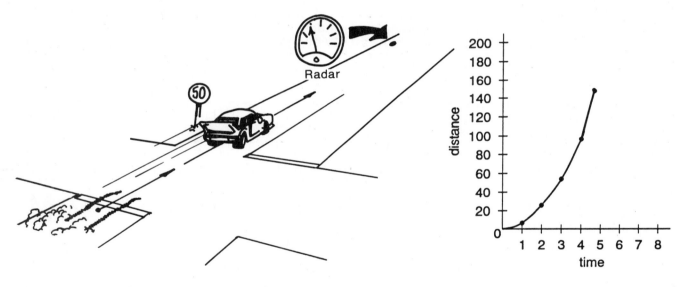

a   Is the Porsche accelerating? Explain your answer.

b   Will the driver of the Porsche get a ticket for speeding if this pattern continues? Explain your answer.

c   Find the equation represented in the table. (Hint: $d = \square t^2$.)

t	d
0	0
1	6
2	24
3	54
4	96
5	150

d Suppose that when $t = 3$ seconds, the driver spots the officer with the radar gun and anxiously looks at the speedometer. (Note that the Porsche's average speed between 2 and 3 seconds is

$$\frac{54 - 24}{1} = 30 \text{ feet/second.)}$$

i Explain why the car's speed during the tenth of a second (0.1 second) before the driver spots the radar trap is

$$\frac{(6 \times 3^2) - (6 \times 2.9^2)}{3 - 2.9} \text{ feet/second.}$$

ii Calculate the speed during this one-tenth of a second. Why is the speed for this "instant" higher than the average speed of 30 feet/second?

iii Complete the following table.

Time Just Before Radar Gun Seen t (seconds)	Distance at Time t (feet)	Time on Seeing Radar Gun (seconds)	Distance When Radar Gun Seen (feet)	Average Speed (feet/second)
2.9	6×2.9^2	3	6×3^2	$\dfrac{(6 \times 3^2) - (6 \times 2.9^2)}{3 - 2.9} = 35.4$
2.99	6×2.99^2	3	6×3^2	
2.999		3	6×3^2	

iv Complete this table by predicting the **average** speeds from patterns you find in the table in problem **d iii**.

Time Before Seeing Officer (seconds)	Average Speed (feet/second)
2.9	35.4
2.99	35.94
2.999	35.994
2.9999	35.9994
2.99999	
2.999999	
2.9999999	
2.99999999	
2.999999999	

v What do you think is the speed of the Porsche when the driver spots the radar gun at *exactly* 3 seconds?

vi Will the driver get a ticket in a 50 miles/hour speed zone? (Use the flowchart if you need to.)

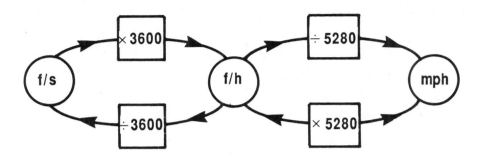

e i Find the speed of the car after exactly 8 seconds using the method in **d** above.

ii Would the Porsche be breaking a 55 miles/hour speed limit after 8 seconds?

2 The *average speed* of a moving object represents its typical speed during a given time interval—not its exact speed. In the following problem, think about why calculating *instantaneous speed* is often more useful than average speed.

A large crane drops a steel ball on a foundation to crush it. The ball drops *d* meters in *t* seconds.

t	d
0	0
1	5
2	20
3	45
4	80

Suppose the concrete foundation will break if the ball reaches a speed of 28 meters/second. The operator needs to know if a ball traveling for 3 seconds will smash the concrete.

a Using the table, come up with the average speed of the ball between 2 and 3 seconds. Remember: $s = \dfrac{\text{change in } d}{\text{change in } t}$

b Find a formula that relates *t* and *d*.

c Now complete this table.

Time Just Before Impact t (seconds)	Distance at Time t (meters)	Time to Impact (seconds)	Distance to Impact (meters)	Average Speed (meters/second)
2.9	5×2.9^2	3	45	29.5
2.99		3	45	
2.999		3	45	

d Predict the ball's speed at *exactly* 3 seconds.

e Will the concrete foundation be smashed if the ball drops for 3 seconds?

f For the operator of the crane, does it matter whether the method from *a* or *d* is used to calculate the ball's speed at 3 seconds? Explain your answer.

3 A child releases the emergency brake of his mother's car. The car hits another car 5 seconds later. The bumpers on both cars will need to be repaired if the speed of collision is more than 24 feet/second. His mother's car moves *d* feet in *t* seconds.

a Find an equation that describes the relationship between *t* and *d* in the table.

b Make a table to show the car's exact speed at 5 seconds.

c Will the bumpers need repair?

t	d
0	0
1	1.5
2	6
3	13.5
4	24

4 After *t* weeks of spring weather, a farmer has *n* fruit flies on her property.

t	n
0	0
1	1,000
2	4,000
3	9,000
4	16,000
5	25,000

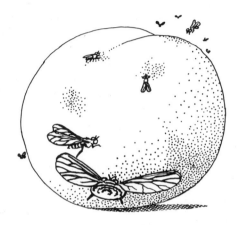

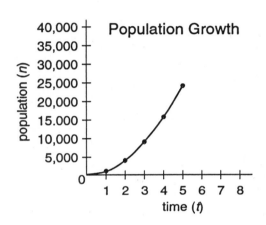

a Find a formula for *n*.

b Make a table and find the *rate* (or speed) at which the fruit fly population is rising when *t* = 6 weeks.

c Predict the size of the population after 100 weeks. Why doesn't this answer make sense?

5 In the following tables, *t* = time, *d* = distance, and *s* = speed.

a Complete the tables and each pair of formulas.

i

t	d	s
0	0	0
1	1	2
2	4	4
3	9	6
4	16	

$$d = \square\, t^{\square}$$
$$s = \square\, t^{\square}$$

ii

t	d	s
0	0	0
1	3	6
2	12	12
3	27	18
4	48	

$$d = \Box\, t^{\Box}$$
$$s = \Box\, t^{\Box}$$

iii

t	d	s
0	0	0
1	0.5	1
2	2	2
3	4.5	
4	8	

$$d = \Box\, t^{\Box}$$
$$s = \Box\, t^{\Box}$$

b What is the relationship between distance and speed in the formulas for **a i–iii**?

c Use the pattern that relates the distance and speed formulas to complete these tables.

i

d	s
t^2	$2t$
$3t^2$	$6t$
$0.5t^2$	t
$5t^2$	$10t$
at^2	

ii

d	s
$11t^2$	
$7t^2$	
$4t^2$	
$20t^2$	
$100t^2$	

iii

d	s
$6t + 4$	6
$11t - 8$	
$14t$	
7	
$bt + c$	

Hint: Consider how the *rate of change* is expressed in a linear equation.

MATHEMATICAL INVESTIGATIONS • DALE SEYMOUR PUBLICATIONS

6 Donna enjoys shooting the rapids on a raft.
She travels *d* meters in *t* seconds.

a Check that $d = \frac{1}{2}t^2 + 3t + 1$ by substitut-

ing pairs of (*t,d*) values from this table.

t	d
0	1.0
1	4.5
2	9.0
3	14.5
4	21.0

b Donna collides with a large rock after 4
seconds.

   i What is the speed of the raft
between *t* = 3.9 and *t* = 4.0 seconds?
(Hint: Remember that

$$d = \frac{1}{2}t^2 + 3t + 1.)$$

   ii Use this information to make a table
(similar to the table in **diii** on p.112)
and find the exact speed at 4
seconds.

Table of Speeds

t	s
0	
1	
2	
3	
4	

c **i** Make four similar tables showing the
exact speed at 0, 1, 2, and 3 seconds.
Use these tables to complete this table
of speeds before Donna's collision (s is
the speed at time *t).*

   ii Look for a pattern in the speed table to
find the equation relating speed and
time.

d Find a speed formula for each of the following distance formulas:

i $d = \frac{1}{2}t^2$

ii $d = 3t$

iii $d = 1$

e If $d = \frac{1}{2}t^2 + 3t + 1$, we know $s = t + 3$ from **c ii**. How can you use your answers in **d** to *quickly* obtain the same result?

7 For each of the following distance formulas, find the related speed equation. In each case, check the equation for the given value of t by using the table method introduced in **1**.

a $d = 5t^2 + 3t + 1$

$$\Downarrow$$

$s = \square t + \triangle + \diamondsuit$

   Check when $t = 5$.

b $d = 3t^2 + 4t + 2$

$$\Downarrow$$

$s = \square t + \triangle + \diamondsuit$

   Check when $t = 2$.

c $d = 4t^2 - 2t - 1$

$$\Downarrow$$

$s = \square - \triangle - \diamondsuit$

   Check when $t = 4$.

8 Sally buys shares in a company when $t = 0$. Her stockbroker uses this formula to predict the price of a share in dollars (p) after t weeks:

$$p = 5.6 + 2t - 0.1t^2.$$

a The broker predicts that the share price will change at a rate of $2 - 0.2t$. Show why.

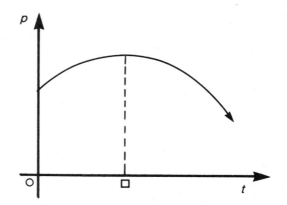

t (weeks)	Rate ($/week)
0	2
2	
4	
6	
8	
10	
12	
14	

b Use the formula in a to help you complete the table.

c Graph the pairs of values in 8 b. What does a negative rate mean?

d i When should Sally sell to maximize her profit?

ii What value of t goes in the box shown on the graph?

e Compare the graph for the price of the shares ($p = 5.6 + 2t - 0.1t^2$) to the rate-of-change graph ($r = 2 - 0.2t$).

ON YOUR OWN

How do stockbrokers come up with formulas to predict share price, such as the one Sally's stockbroker used in problem 8? Ask a stockbroker, financial planner, or mathematician in your community.

9 In a race, suppose it takes a champion 4 seconds to reach her top speed of 9 meters/second. She runs *d* meters in *t* seconds at a speed of *s* meters/second. The line on the graph shows how her speed increases and then becomes constant over time.

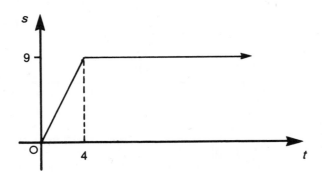

a Show that $d = 1.125t^2$ when $t \leq 4$ fits the information on the graph.

b **i** How far has she run when $t = 4$?

ii Show that the formula for the runner's distance is $d = 9t - 18$ when $t \geq 4$.

Investigation Four

Maxima and Minima

1 A show-off flexes his muscles at the county fair by trying to ring the bell on a test-of-strength game. When he hits the pad, the weight jumps h meters above its starting position in t seconds.

a Suppose a physicist says that $h = 5t - 5t^2$. Complete the table.

b **i** At what time (t) is the weight at its maximum height? Make a graph to help explain why.

 ii Find the weight's maximum height.

c **i** Suppose s is the speed of the weight at time t. Complete the related speed equation:

$$h = 5t - 5t^2$$
$$\Downarrow$$
$$s = \square - \square t$$

 ii What is the speed of the weight at the maximum height?

 iii Use the speed equation to find the time (t) when the weight reaches its maximum height. Make a graph of the speed at each time to show the value of t when $s = 0$. How are the two graphs related?

d If $h = 10t - 5t^2$ for another contestant, find the maximum height of the weight.

e Which method is easier for finding the maximum height—using table patterns or the speed formula?

t	h
0	0
0.2	0.8
0.4	
0.6	
0.8	
1.0	

2 An arrow is shot straight up in the air. It is *h* meters high in *t* seconds.

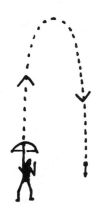

t	h
0	0
2	40
4	40
6	0

a Substitute pairs of (*t, h*) values from the table to show that $h = 30t - 5t^2$.

b Find the speed formula.

c Find the time at the maximum height.

d Find the maximum height.

3 Find the maximum distance from the starting point in each case.

a $d = 6t - 2t^2$

c $d = 8 + 6t - 2t^2$

b $d = 60t - 10t^2$

d $d = 11 + 60t - 10t^2$

4 A yo-yo drops and rises again. It is *h* meters from the ground at time *t* seconds.

t	h
0	1
0.2	0.4
0.8	1

a Show that $h = 5t^2 - 4t + 1$ represents the values in the table.

b Find the speed formula.

c When does the yo-yo stop moving?

d Find the minimum height above the ground that the yo-yo can reach.

5 Find the minimum distance above the ground from the starting point in each case.

a $d = 2t^2 - 4t + 10$

b $d = 3t^2 - 18t + 30$

c $d = t^2 - 8t + 21$

d $d = 4t^2 - 2t + 3$

6 All of the problems in this investigation so far have used speed formulas for an object–such as the arrow problem in **a** below. However, you can also find formulas that do not represent speed–as in **b** below.

   a If $d = 20t - t^2$ represents the movement of an arrow, find the maximum distance d and the time t when the arrow is at its highest point.

   b Ace Architects design a simple rectangular house with a perimeter of 40 meters. They wonder what dimensions will create a rectangular house with maximum floor area.

   $A\ m^2$ y meters

   x meters

   Complete the table.

x (length)	y (width)	Pattern in y
0	20	$20 - 0$
1	19	$20 - 1$
2	18	
3		
4		
x		$20 - \square$

   c i Explain why $A = x(20 - x)$.

   ii Show that $A = 20x - x^2$.

   d Look at your answers to **a**. Change distance (d) and time (t) in the formula to represent x and A: $A = 20x - x^2$. Now calculate the maximum area and the values of x and y when this occurs. What is the shape of the floor that has the largest area?

7 In establishing pairs of equations such as the ones in this investigation, the key consideration is the *relationship* between the quadratic equation and the linear equation. These pairs of equations relate *three* quantities—for example, distance, time, and speed.

   a Why is one equation quadratic and the other linear?

b A farmer has 200 yards of electric fence to enclose his cows. He makes a rectangle by using an existing fence as one of the four sides. He wants to maximize the area of his pasture.

i Complete the table.

x (length)	y (width)	Pattern in y
0	200	$200 - (2 \times 0)$
10	180	$200 - (2 \times 10)$
20	160	
30		
40		
x	y	$200 - (2 \times \square)$

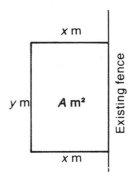

ii Show that $A = 200x - 2x^2$.

iii Show that the area is at its maximum when $x = 50$ yards. Find y and A for the maximum case.

iv How are the answers for **iii** related to the numbers that go into the empty boxes on this graph?

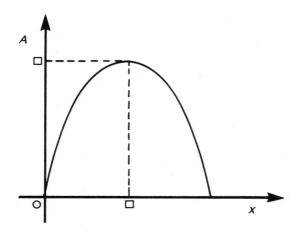

8 Player Window Company makes aluminum window frames by using a total of 800 centimeters of framing. Each window has four vertical pieces and two horizontal pieces.

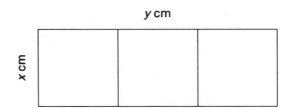

---

x (horizontal)	y (vertical)	Pattern in y
0	400	
10	380	
20		400 − (2 × 20)
30		
40		
x	y	400 − (2 × ☐)

a   Complete the table.

b   If A cm^2 is the area of the window, show that $A = 400x - 2x^2$.

c   Find the area and dimensions of the window that has the maximum area.

9   AmAir will sell n tickets by charging $\$c$ per ticket. The plane can carry 380 passengers.

c (dollars)	n (tickets)	Pattern in n
150	380	680 − (2 × 150)
160	360	680 − (2 × 160)
170	340	
180		
190		
c	n	680 − (☐ × c)

a   Complete the table.

b   If $\$T$ = total revenue, show that $T = 680c - 2c^2$.

c   Why should AmAir charge $170 to maximize their revenue? Explain your answer.

ON YOUR OWN

Why do you think so many natural phenomena can be represented by quadratic equations? Ask a science or math teacher—or an engineer in your community—about this. Make a list of real-world situations that can be described by a quadratic equation.

CHECK-UP

1 Firewood costs $c for *n* bags.

    a Write a formula for *c* to fit each firewood advertisement.

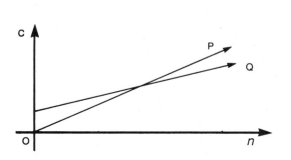

GREENWOOD RECREATION
———————
$7.00 per bag   *plus*   *$9.00 for delivery*

NORFOLK FIREWOOD SUPPLIES
$8.50 per bag   including   delivery

    b The graph shows the two formulas in **a**. Match the graphs with the companies.

    c **i** When does Rex buy from Greenwood Recreation because it is the best deal?

       ii Under what conditions would he choose Norfolk Firewood Supplies instead?

2 Miriam and her friends have fun on the giant waterslide. Miriam slides *d* meters in *t* seconds.

t	*d*
0	0
1	3
2	12
3	27
4	48

    a The table shows how far Miriam traveled in the first 4 seconds. Write the equation that represents Miriam's distance and time.

    b What was her average speed during the fourth second?

    c Find the speeds in short-time intervals before $t = 4$ to show that Miriam's exact speed at $t = 4$ is 24 meters/second.

3 Jeff is in a car that has traveled d feet in t seconds.

a Check that $d = t^2 + 16t - 32$.

b Show that his speed at 6 seconds is 28 feet/second.

c Complete the speed formula where s is the speed at time t.

t	d
4	48
5	73
6	100

4 Debbie makes a rectangular vegetable garden by using the corner of two perpendicular fences. She uses 17 square paving stones to make a pathway along the other two sides of her garden. Each paving stone is 1 foot × 1 foot.

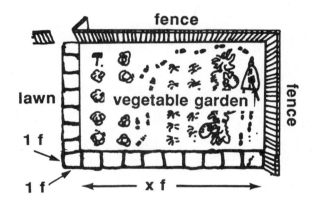

Debbie wonders what length and width of paving stones will give her rectangular vegetable garden the maximum area.

a i If x feet is the length of the plot and A feet^2 is the area, explain why $A = x(16 - x)$.

ii Show that $A = 16x - x^2$.

b Find the dimensions for the maximum garden area. Draw a diagram that shows the fences and Debbie's arrangement of the paving stones.

CHAPTER FIVE

Using Maps

TEACHING NOTES

This chapter investigates various features and applications of maps. Topics addressed include orienteering, calculating the shortest route between points on the globe, exploring time zones, and an introduction to celestial navigation. Though maps are included in the materials, it would be helpful to have a collection of maps and globes for students to use for this series of investigations. For example, good backpacking topographical maps are produced by the U. S. Geological Survey (U.S.G.S.) in 1 to 24,000 and 1 to 62,500 scales— that is, one foot on the map equals 24,000 or 62,500 feet on the ground—for most areas in the United States. The area between contour lines on these maps represents 40-foot and 80-foot changes in altitude respectively.

In addition, be sure there are globes for students to work with. You may want to review (or introduce) terms such as *longitude, meridian, latitude,* and *Greenwich Mean Time* before students work on Investigations Three and Four. In particular, some students may need to review notation for the 24-hour clock used to show Greenwich Mean Time.

Investigation One • Orienteering

Topographical maps are used by backpackers, forestry workers, scientists, and the military to help with planning and navigation for cross-country journeys. U.S.G.S. topographical maps are available in several scales, depending on how much detail is required—(and how much paper you want to carry. Typically, hikers use 1:24,000 scale maps, which show 7.5 minutes of latitude and longitude and 40 feet of altitude between pairs of contour lines.

The sport of *orienteering* requires the accurate use of a compass and experience with topographical maps. The goal of orienteering is to navigate a course through unfamiliar terrain in a limited period of time. In this investigation, students interpret topographical maps and sketch views of a scene from various perspectives.

Investigation Two • Shortest Routes

Mercator projection maps are constructed by projecting a globe on a surrounding cylinder. Students learn to find the shortest distance between points on the surface of a cylinder and cube by unfolding the paper model and using a ruler to measure the distance.

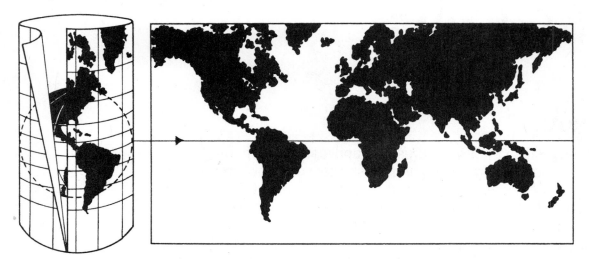

An *azimuthal projection* is made by projecting any hemisphere (not only the obvious ones such as the northern or southern hemispheres but any slice through the center of the earth) onto a place that touches the hemisphere at its "pole," or highest point. This process produces a circular map. The polar equidistant projection is the most common example of an azimuthal projection. In such a projection, the shortest distance from a pole to any point on the surface of the hemisphere is found by drawing a straight line from the pole to the point. The true distance is then calculated by using the linear scale provided with the map.

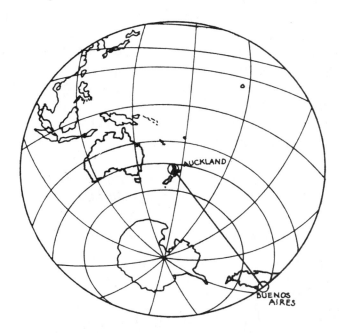

The shortest route between two locations on a polar equidistant map (also called the *Great Circle* route) is usually shown by the straight line joining the points—provided the line passes through or very near the pole. For example, in problem 6 the line joining Anchorage to Oslo is very nearly the shortest route. However, for two points on the equator, the Great Circle route is the equator itself, which is shown as the outside circle on a polar equidistant map. Therefore, a straight-line journey between two points near the equator does not indicate the shortest route on this type of map.

The map in problem 7 shows Auckland, New Zealand, at the "pole" of the azimuthal map. Therefore, the shortest route from Auckland to any other point on the map can be found by connecting the two locations with a straight line. Since every point on the earth's surface can be represented as the pole of an azimuthal map, there are an infinite number of possible maps.

While azimuthal maps can provide the Great Circle routes, in practice an airplane flight following such a route requires a continual change in bearing, which is impossible without the use of computer-flight controls. In contrast, Mercator maps are much easier to use as a navigational aid, since a constant compass bearing will navigate a pilot to a destination. Mercator routes are only suitable for short flights, however, since they do not follow the Great Circle route (the shortest distance between two points on the earth). For long flights, the difference in length between a Mercator route and Great Circle route is significant—as students will discover as they work through the problems in this investigation.

Investigation Three • Longitude

Greenwich Mean Time (GMT) is introduced as a standard upon which world time is based. The prime meridian is the 0° line of longitude that passes through Greenwich, England. Since there are 24 hours in a day, there are 24 time zones. Each 15° longitude to the east increases GMT time by one hour, and each 15° west decreases GMT by one hour. (Note that 360 ÷ 24 = 15.) Therefore, the sun takes four minutes to pass over 1° of longitude.

Activities in this section include calculating *true local time* (TLT) of a city based on the number of degrees longitude it is east or west of the prime meridian.

For west longitude x, TLT = GMT $- \dfrac{x}{15}$; For east longitude y, TLT = GMT $+ \dfrac{y}{15}$.

In other words, the true local time is earlier than GMT if you're west of Greenwich (compare New York City and London, for example)—and it's later if you're east of Greenwich (compare London and Delhi).

It is also possible to calculate the longitude of your location on the earth if you know the current TLT and GMT. For example, if the TLT in Dakar, Africa, is 07:44 hour, and GMT is 09:00 hours, the difference is 76 minutes. The longitude of Dakar is then 76 ÷ 4, or 19°W. In this example, the TLT is earlier than GMT and therefore west of the prime meridian.

Since true local time changes constantly as you move around the earth, the notion of time zones is introduced as a way to help local communities schedule events. Otherwise, every city along a latitude would have a different noon. Students also explore using the time of the local *solar noon* (when the sun is at its highest point) and that of the Greenwich Solar Noon (GSN) in order to find the longitude of a city. This is similar to the previous calculation of longitude but a simple graph gives the Greenwich Solar Noon time for all dates of the year, therefore eliminating the need to know the GMT.

Investigation Four • Navigating by the Stars

Students are introduced to celestial navigation in this section. Since the star Polaris is positioned directly over the North Pole, simple geometry shows that the angle between the horizon and Polaris is equal to the the latitude of the observer. For centuries travelers have used the position of Polaris to locate their latitude and "true north." Knowing this information has allowed sailors to navigate across oceans where no other points of reference were available. In the southern hemisphere, where Polaris is below the horizon, the Southern Cross constellation is used to locate the *celestial south pole*—an imaginary point directly above the south pole. This point allowed sailors to navigate in the southern seas.

Students learn about the sextant, a protractor of sorts that measures the angle of inclination of stars above the horizon. If you observe the star Polaris at 40° above the horizon (its angle of inclination), you are on latitude 40°. However, even with this reading, your longitude could be anywhere. To get a location "fix" (latitude *and* longitude), you need to measure the inclination of a second star. Find Polaris and a second star (for example, Alpha Centauri) in the night sky. Then use a nautical almanac that gives information about the positions of stars at any time of the year. With this information, you can "fix" your position on the earth.

In problem 5 of this investigation, Hannah uses the following procedure to fix her position. You may want to look over the diagrams there as visual aids.

How to Do a Two-Star Fix:

In the nautical almanac table for Alpha Centauri, look up the current time. The table will give the latitude and longitude of the point on the surface of the earth directly below the star at that moment. The point is called the *geographical position* (GP) of the star and changes continuously as the earth rotates. The GP for Alpha Centauri is what the north pole is for Polaris. Therefore, a sextant reading of 50° between Alpha Centauri and the horizon locates the user on the "latitude" of 50° relative to the GP "pole" of Alpha Centauri (this latitude will be tilted relative to the normal latitudes). You are located on the 50° "latitude" (circle) for Alpha Centauri, as well as on the 40° latitude for Polaris. These two circles intersect at two points that are actually far apart. Since you'll have a reasonable idea of your actual location, it should be obvious which point is correct. However, you could follow the same procedure and find a third star to remove all doubt about which of the two points is the true location.

Note that it will be extremely difficult for students to grasp the notion of a two-star location fix without practical experience using a globe, some string or wire latitude circles, and a protractor.

Investigation One

Orienteering

1   Topographical maps show a top view of the terrain with concentric *contour* lines indicating a change in ground height—or altitude. The sport of orienteering involves using a topographical map and compass to travel from point to point over unfamiliar terrain in a limited time period.

Kathleen is on an orienteers course in the mountains. She reaches a lookout position and sees this view.

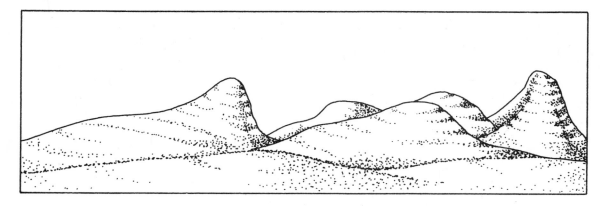

Her topographical map of the area looks like this. It shows a change of 100 feet in ground height between each pair of contour lines.

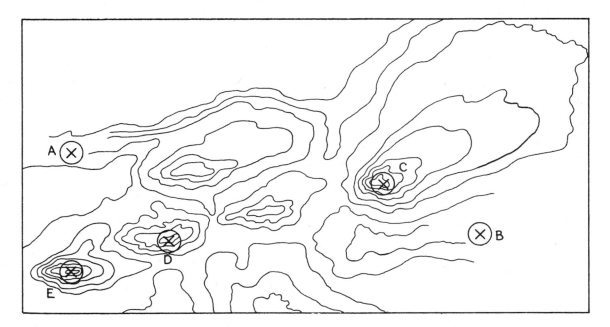

a Kathleen is sure her map is upside down. Why does she think this?

b Checkpoints for the orienteers course that Kathleen runs are at A, B, C, D, and E. Draw a sketch of the view that Kathleen will see when she reaches the following checkpoints:

i A

ii B

iii C

2 On this topographical map, the height difference between adjacent contours is 40 feet.

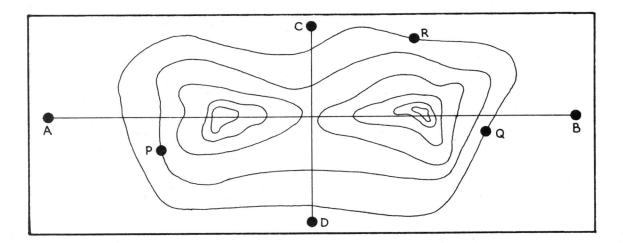

a Draw diagrams to show the views from A, B, C, and D.

b Describe the easiest walking route from:

i P to Q.

ii P to R.

ON YOUR OWN

This map show contours that are 50 feet apart. The scale is 1 inch = 1 mile.

1 Draw what the area looks like from at least two views on the ground.

2 Draw an enlargement of the topographical map.

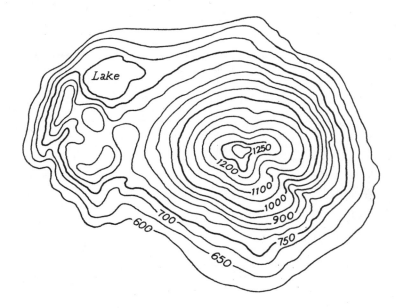

3 Cut along the 600-foot contour line and use the map as a template to transfer the 600-foot contour to a piece of corrugated cardboard or foam. Cut out the cardboard contour.

4 Repeat **3** using the contours for 650 feet, 700 feet, and so on.

5 Glue the contour "sheets" together to make a model of the mountain.

3 Six checkpoints are marked on this topographical map.

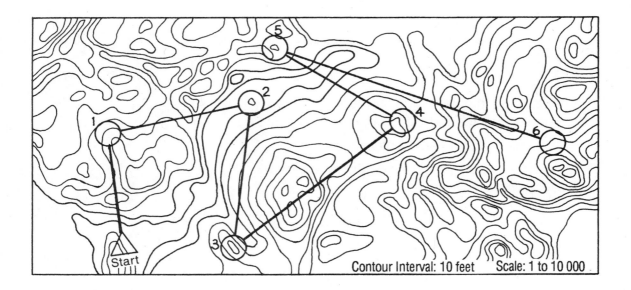

Contour Interval: 10 feet   Scale: 1 to 10 000

a Draw a diagram to show the changes in altitude for a direct journey from the start to checkpoint 1.

b Draw similar diagrams to show the following direct journeys:

   i   1 to 2.

   ii 2 to 3.

   iii 3 to 4.

   iv 4 to 5.

c David knows that it usually doesn't make sense to walk in straight lines when orienteering. Plan a more sensible route for David to visit checkpoints 1 through 6.

4 Maps generally indicate *true north,* the direction of the north pole, or *grid north,* an adjusted north that results from projecting the globe onto a flat grid of latitude and longitude lines. Orienteering topographical maps, however, also indicate *magnetic north*—north as indicated by a compass.

a Find out why orienteering maps always indicate magnetic north.

b Why are grid north and true north different?

c Find out how to use an orienteering compass.

ON YOUR OWN

The maps used in orienteering competitions have much more detail than just contour information.

1 Study an example of an orienteering map.

2 Find out the strategies good orienteers use to cover a course quickly.

Investigation Two

Shortest Routes

1   The following diagrams show one way to make a map of the world.

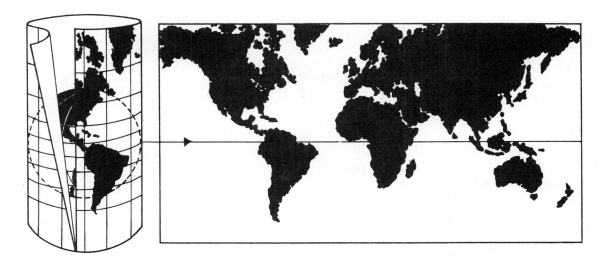

The globe is projected by an imaginary light at the earth's center onto a cylinder touching the globe at the equator. The cylinder is then laid flat. The projection of the globe onto the cylinder is known as the *Mercator Projection*.

a   Why do Mercator maps of the world usually lie within latitudes of about 80°N and 60°S?

b   Greenland has an area of about 2.2 million kilometers², while Australia's area is about 7.7 million kilometers². Explain why Greenland appears to be larger than Australia on a Mercator projection.

2   Arturo lives on a strange world shaped like a Mercator cylinder. When he boards a flight from A to B, he notices that the flight-information magazine shows the route on a flat map as a straight line joining A and B.

a   Mark A and B on a rectangular piece of paper. Roll the paper to make a cylinder and tape the edge. Note what the shortest route looks like on the cylinder world.

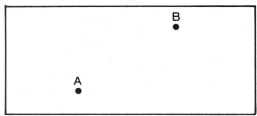

b The second leg of Arturo's journey takes him from B to C.

    i Mark point C on the cylinder below and to the right of B.

    ii Cut along a vertical line XY between B and C to again form a flat map.

    iii Show the shortest route from B to C on this map.

    iv Why is your map not suitable for finding the shortest routes?

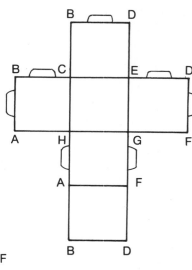

c On Mercator projection maps of the world, is the cut in the cylinder always made in the same place? For example, if you lived in New Zealand or Turkey, do you think your world map would look exactly like an American-made map?

3 An ant lives on the surface of a hollow cube.

a Copy the flat-box diagram onto graph paper and make a cube. (Include flaps on alternate edges and label the corners.)

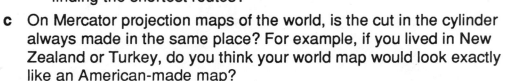

b The ant journeys from A to D.

    i Make another copy of the flat-box diagram and, while unfolded, mark the ant's shortest route from A to D.

    ii Mark the shortest route from A to E on the unfolded diagram.

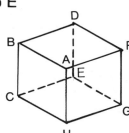

c Fold the marked diagram into a cube. Note where both shortest routes you marked in **b** are.

d What is the length of the longest straight-line route that the ant can walk on the cube?

4 a To make a cone, cut a *sector* from a flat circle and tape the circle at the cut. Explore how to make cones by drawing diagrams that include:

    i tall cones with small bases.

    ii low cones with large bases.

b Suppose Mt. Fuji in Japan closely approximates a cone. An engineer plans the shortest road between two positions on the mountain. Explain how to find shortest routes on cones.

5 a Explain how to find the shortest ant-walking distance between any two points on the fan.

b If a shape can be made out of a flat piece of paper, how can you always find the shortest distance between two points on the paper?

*O*N YOUR OWN

1 An engineer designs a belt-drive system with a belt in the form of a Möbius strip.

    a Make a Möbius strip.

    b Use a pencil to show that your strip has only one side.

    c Explain the engineer's reasoning for designing the belt in the form of a Möbius strip.

2 Explain how to find the shortest distance between two points on a Möbius strip.

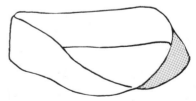

3 a Use scissors to cut along a center line (parallel to the edges) of your Möbius strip. Describe the result.

    b Predict the result of cutting another Möbius strip along two lines parallel to the edges. Check your prediction.

6 This *polar equidistant map* is an example of an *azimuthal projection map.* Such projections are commonly used to show the Arctic and Antarctic regions but can also represent any hemisphere (half) of the globe. That means the "pole"—or center—of an azimuthal map does not have to be the north or south pole.

a Find out what azimuthal means.

b A pilot plans to fly from Anchorage in Alaska to Oslo in Norway, so she joins the two cities on the map with a straight line.

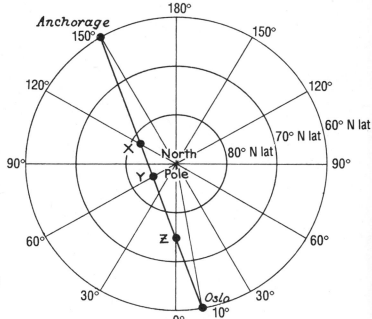

i Use a piece of string and a globe to check that her route is very close to the shortest route.

ii Use a protractor to measure the plane's *bearing*—the angle between the flight path and a line from the North Pole—at points *X, Y,* and *Z* along the route.

iii Why will the pilot find it difficult to follow the direct route marked on the map? (Hint: Look at your answers to **ii**.)

c This diagram shows another route the pilot could have taken if she had used a Mercator map.

i What are the bearings at points U, V, and W along the flight path? What do you notice about these bearings compared to those in **b ii**?

ii Will the pilot find the Mercator map easier to use for navigation? Explain your answer.

d i On a copy of the azimuthal map, sketch the Mercator route from Anchorage to Oslo. Use the bearing information in **c i** to help you locate the flight path.

ii Mark the positions of points U, V, and W on your azimuthal map.

iii On the azimuthal map, is the route along U, V, and W longer or shorter than the X, Y, and Z route?

e List the advantages and disadvantages of using an azimuthal or a Mercator map for navigation near either pole.

7 An Aerolineas Argentina 747 jet is about to depart from Auckland in New Zealand on a nonstop flight to Buenos Aires in Argentina. The pilot has an azimuthal map that shows Auckland at the center "pole." The shortest route to *any* other place from Auckland is found by drawing a straight line between the cities.

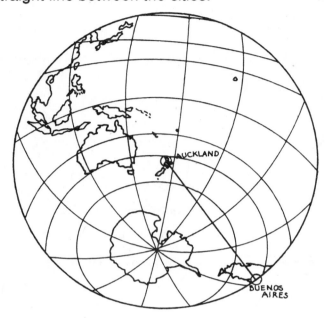

a i On a globe of the world, stretch a piece of string between Auckland and Buenos Aires to find the shortest route. This forms part of a *Great Circle* that would go completely around the world and return to Auckland (its origin).

ii Does your string on the globe follow the same route as the flight path on the azimuthal map?

b i Using this Mercator map, draw a straight flight path from Auckland to Buenos Aires.

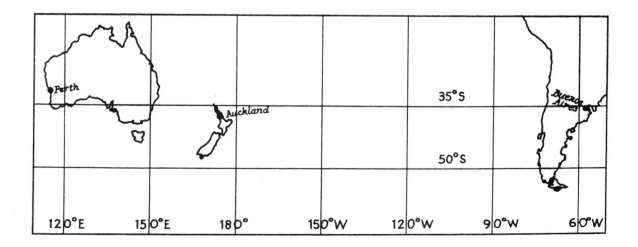

    ii Compare the length of this flight path with the Great Circle route on a globe. Which is the fuel-efficient route?

c Will a straight line from Perth in Western Australia to Buenos Aires on this azimuthal map represent the shortest route? Check your answer by using a piece of string and a globe.

---

*O*N YOUR OWN

1   Use a copy of a Mercator world map.

2   With a globe and string, find the shortest routes from the international airport near you to your three favorite cities in the world.

3   Carefully sketch these shortest routes on your Mercator map.

4   Do planes actually fly the shortest routes from your airport? What could cause pilots to use a longer, nonstop route?

Investigation Three

Longitude

1 Longitude 0° is an imaginary north-south line connecting both poles and passing through Greenwich, England. This line is also called the *prime meridian.*

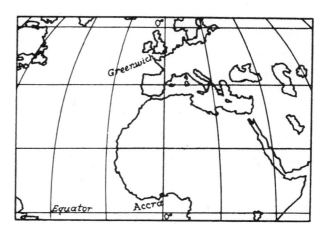

a Find out why longitude 0° was originally established at the former Royal Observatory in Greenwich Park in a borough of London. (The Royal Greenwich Observatory is now at Herstmonceux, Surrey.)

b If the time at Greenwich, England is 08:40 hours in Greenwich Mean Time (GMT), what is the time in Accra, Ghana, in Africa? Explain your answer.

c Explain the meaning of each of the following:

   i meridian.

   ii A.M.

   iii P.M.

d Vince knows that where he lives the *true local time* (TLT) is one hour later than in Greenwich, England. Therefore, Vince knows he lives 15° east of Greenwich. Explain his reasoning.

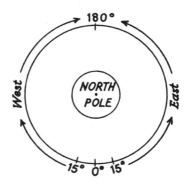

e Complete the tables on the next page for Greenwich Mean Time (GMT) 19:00 on a Tuesday. (Note: If you don't know how to convert GMT hours to clock time, find out how to do so.)

i   **West of Greenwich**

Longitude*(x)*	True Local Time *(t)*	Clock Time
0°	19:00 Tuesday (GMT)	7:00 P.M.
15°	18:00 Tuesday	6:00 P.M.
30°		
45°		
60°		
75°		
90°		
105°		
120°		
135°		
150°		
165°		
180°		
195°		

ii   **East of Greenwich**

Longitude*(y)*	True Local Time *(t)*	Clock Time
0°	19:00 Tuesday (GMT)	7:00 P.M.
15°	20:00 Tuesday	8:00 P.M.
30°		
45°		
60°		
75°		
90°		
105°		
120°		
135°		
150°		
165°		
180°		
195°		

f i Use your answers in problem **e** to explain why we need an *international date line.*

ii On the first table, why is 195° at 6:00 A.M. on Wednesday? On the second table, why is 195° at 8:00 A.M. on Tuesday?

g Use the table in **e i** to write an equation that relates the degrees *west* of the prime meridian and TLT. If you know that your true local time is 17:48 hours (assume GMT is still 19:00), use this equation to prove that you must live on longitude 18° west of Greenwich.

h Use the table in **e ii** to write a formula that relates the degrees *east* of the prime meridian and TLT.

i Use the east and west longitude formulas to complete these tables. (Assume GMT and TLT are on the same day.)

i

GMT	TLT	Longitude
09:00	07:44	
14:30	17:26	
12:00	18:36	
23:45	21:01	
16:38	10:22	

ii

GMT	TLT	Longitude
12:00		6° E
14:00		36° W
13:30		58° E
	12:00	120° W
	12:00	120° E

2 The continental United States lies between longitudes 67°W and 124°W.

a If GMT is 12:00 (noon),

i what is the range of true local times in the United States?

ii If you include all 50 states, what is the range of true local times in the United States? Explain why.

iii Is there a place in the United States that has the same true local time as Auckland, New Zealand?

b Is it true that if you travel east to west you would have to continuously change your watch to determine the true local time? Explain your answer.

On YOUR OWN

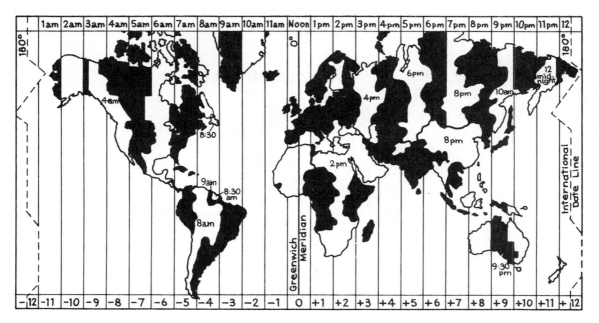

Here is a time zone map of the world. Compare it with a world map that shows the borders of the countries. Explain why there are irregularities in the time zones.

3 A jet leaves Melbourne, Australia (Point M on the map), longitude 145°E, at GMT 12:00 Friday to fly via Antarctica to Rio de Janeiro (Point R), longitude 43°W.

a Calculate the difference between the true local times in the two cities.

b Compare your answer in **a** to the answer obtained using the world time zone map above.

c Explain why the jet rapidly changes time zones near the south pole.

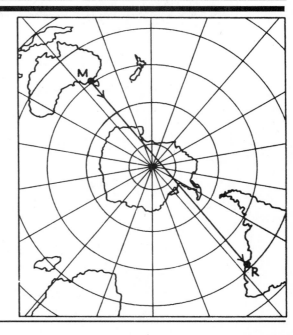

4 Until the invention of very accurate clocks, it was impossible to calculate the longitude of a ship at sea.

a Use a map showing the Atlantic Ocean to investigate this navigational advice given to captains before such a clock was available.

> *To get to the West Indies from Britain, head south until the butter melts, then sail due west.*

b A clipper ship sails from London, England, in March 1852 for Sydney, Australia, with a very accurate clock on board set for GMT. At noon on April 15 of that year, the sun is at its highest point over Greenwich at 12:00 GMT. On the ship, the navigator noted the sun was highest at 07:28 GMT. Show that the longitude of the sailing ship is 68°E.

c Suppose the clock, unknown to the navigator, had actually lost one minute a day and the ship had been sailing for four weeks. Show that the longitude of the ship is 75°E, not 68°E.

d In 1713, the British Government offered a prize of £20,000 (now worth well over $1,000,000) for a clock accurate enough for navigation. The prize was claimed in 1773 by John Harrison after more than thirty years of work. Explain the importance of such a clock to governments at that time.

ON YOUR OWN

Knowing the time (GMT) accurately is still vital for navigation. Accurate time signals are broadcast continuously by stations WWV in Fort Collins, Colorado, and WWVH on Kauai, Hawaii. Both stations broadcast on the radio frequencies 2.5, 5, 10, 15, and 20 MHz.

1 Locate the standard time signal on a short-wave radio and describe how the two stations can be distinguished from each other.

2 Find out about Universal Time (UT).

5 Julie believes the sun is always highest in the sky at 12:00. Jonathan uses the following information printed in the daily paper and estimates that *solar noon*—the time when the sun reaches its highest point in the sky—is actually at 12:23.

SUN, MOON, TIDES
SUN
Today: rises, 6:53 A.M.; sets, 5:53 P.M.
Tomorrow: rises, 6:52 A.M.; sets, 5:54 P.M.
✱✱✱✱✱✱

MOON

---

a Explain Julie's reasoning.

b Explain Jonathan's reasoning.

c Who is correct?

ON YOUR OWN

1 At around 11:30 A.M. local time, fix a stick in a vertical position on a flat sidewalk or driveway.

2 Using chalk, mark the time of the position of the end of the shadow every five minutes.

3 Estimate the time of solar noon from your readings.

4 From the local newspaper or a nautical almanac, work out the time of solar noon and compare this with your answer in **3**.

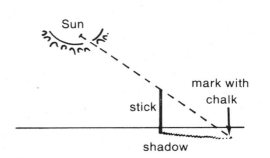

d When will solar noon occur tomorrow?

6 The following graph will help you find the time of solar noon at Greenwich compared with GMT noon.

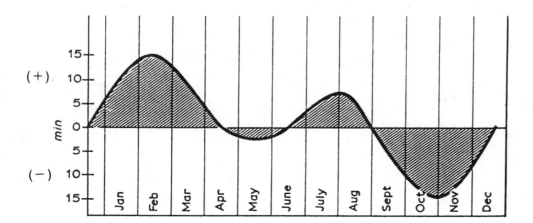

On about April 15, the solar noon is the same as GMT noon.

a List the other three days of the year when this occurs.

b Using the graph, show that solar noon at Greenwich on November 23 occurs at about 11:50 GMT.

c Find the approximate time of solar noon at Greenwich on the following days:

  i February 12.

  ii April 1.

  iii June 30.

  iv October 1.

d A sailor in the middle of the Indian Ocean observes the sun is highest at 08:27 GMT on February 12.

  i What time is the solar noon at Greenwich on February 12?

  ii Show that the difference between the solar noon for the sailor and Greenwich is 3 hours and 48 minutes on February 12.

  iii From **ii**, show the sailor's longitude is 57°E.

e Complete the table for ships in various parts of the world.

Date at Greenwich	Local Solar Noon (GMT)	Greenwich Solar Noon (GMT) on this Date	Difference	Longitude (Nearest Degree)
February 12	08:27	12:15	3 hours, 48 minutes	57°E
April 15	08:00			
July 31	21:07			
September 1	03:05			
October 31	00:02			
May 15	22:41			
March 15	12:04			
January 31	00:47			

f i Look at the graph on page 151. What do you notice about the total area shaded above the horizontal axis compared with the total area shaded below the axis?

ii On average, at what time is the sun at its highest point at Greenwich?

iii Use your answer in **ii** to explain the origin of the term "Greenwich Mean Time."

ON YOUR OWN

Even though Boston and Philadelphia are in the same time zone, they have different true local times.

1 Find the longitudes of these cities on a map.

2 Find the solar noons for each city on October 31 (expressed in GMT). Note: Use the graph in problem **6**.

3 Convert these GMTs in **2** to Eastern Standard Time. Note: Use the time zone map on page 148.

4 Repeat **1** and **2** for Chicago and Dallas, then convert the GMTs to Central Standard Time.

5 Predict when solar noon will be on July 4 for the longitude on which you live.

Investigation Four

Navigating by the Stars

1 Christopher Columbus set out from Spain to find a westward route to East Asia. At that time, there was no way of finding the longitude of the position of a ship, but finding the latitude was well-known. Navigators learned to use the position of special stars to calculate the latitude of their position. Suppose Columbus tried to travel along a given latitude from Spain (about 37°N).

a When Columbus found the West Indies, he thought he had reached Japan. Why was this a reasonable assumption at that time? (Look at a world map.)

b If Columbus was trying to follow latitude 37°N, did his ship stray off course?

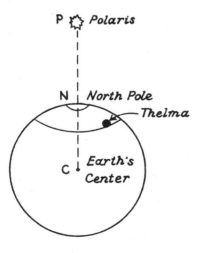

2 Thelma lives in England and she looks at Polaris, the North Star. In the sketch of the earth and Polaris, points P, N, and C lie in a straight line.

a i Will Polaris change position in the night sky, or will it remain fixed? (Spin a globe or soccer ball to help you find out.)

ii How will all other stars appear to Thelma as she watches the night sky for several hours? Will any other stars appear stationary to observers in the northern hemisphere?

iii How could Polaris be used to help sailors navigate on the open sea? What is a possible problem with this technique?

b i The nearest star is about four light years from earth. Light travels at 300,000 kilometers/second. How far is the nearest star from the earth in kilometers?

ii Explain why light rays from *any* star appear parallel when they arrive at the earth.

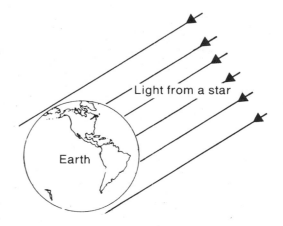

Light from a star

Earth

c Latitudes vary from 0° at the equator to 90° at the poles. Latitude is really the measure of the central angle at the center of the earth. This cross-section of the globe illustrates that the angle *y* represents the latitude of the position on the earth's surface. North and South (N and S) designate whether the position is north or south of the equator.

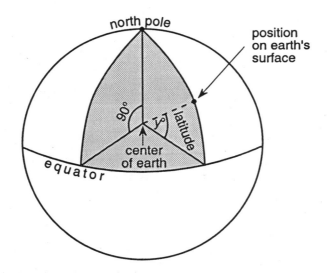

north pole

position on earth's surface

90°

y°

latitude

center of earth

equator

MATHEMATICAL INVESTIGATIONS • DALE SEYMOUR PUBLICATIONS

A ship's navigator uses a *sextant* (a type of protractor) to measure the angle x between the horizon and Polaris.

On this diagram, the latitude of the ship's position P is $y°$.

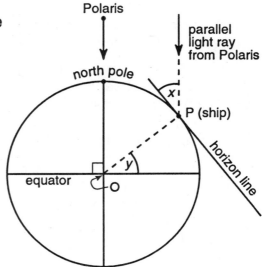

i Show that the measure of the central angle y equals angle x between the horizon line and Polaris.

ii If you were at the north pole, where would Polaris be in the sky? What would your latitude be? Explain your answer.

3 Paul notices that a particular star passes directly over his house each night. Later in the evening, he points directly overhead where the star was earlier. Then he sweeps his arm to point at the current position of the star and continues to sweep straight down to the horizon. He believes his arm is now pointing due west. Use a globe to help you explain Paul's reasoning.

On YOUR OWN

Some researchers believe the Polynesians may have used the method in **3** to help navigate on east-west journeys from one small island to another.

1 Discuss the difficulties and dangers involved.

2 Investigate other Polynesian navigation techniques that use such things as knowledge of

   a wind directions.

   b swell directions.

   c migration of birds pointing to distant lands.

   d other signs of an island being nearby.

4 a On a globe, use circles made from heavy string or wire that exactly fit on latitudes 30°, 40°, 50°, and 60°.

b A navigator on a ship observes Polaris at an angle of 30° above the horizon. Use the appropriate string to show all the places on earth the ship might be.

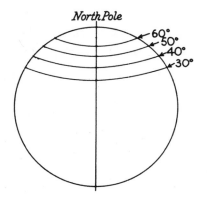

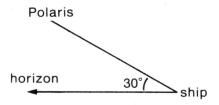

5 a Hannah uses a sextant to work out that her latitude is 60°N by measuring the angle of Polaris above the horizon. Place the 60°- latitude circle you made in **4** on the globe at latitude 60°N to show all her possible locations.

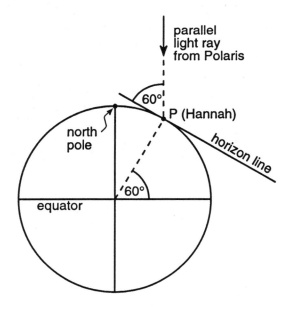

b Hannah reads in her nautical almanac that at 22:00 GMT, a certain star reaches its highest point overhead (its *zenith*) above 180°W, 15°N—a position near Hawaii. Locate this point on your globe and mark it.

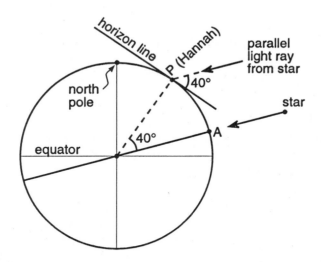

c At 22:00 GMT Hannah observes this star 40° above the horizon. Place the string circle you made for latitude 40° in **4** on your globe (it will be somewhat tilted) so that the center of the string circle is at 180°W, 15°N. Explain why Hannah must be at some point on this circle.

d Hannah could be at either of two possible positions on earth. They are points P and X on this diagram of the two intersecting latitude circles. Note that one circle (60°N) has the north pole (N) as its center. The other circle (40°) has position A as its center—the point where the star is directly overhead.

In practice, it is obvious which position is the correct one (P). Explain why.

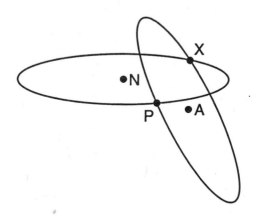

6 The *Geographical Position* (GP) of a star is the place on earth where a star is directly overhead (at its zenith).

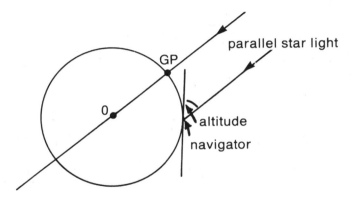

The angle of elevation between the horizon and the star at a particular moment is called its *altitude*. Use your globe and latitude strings to find the positions indicated by the following sightings and information.

Altitude		Geographical Position	
First Star	**Second Star**	**First Star**	**Second Star**
60°	40°	North Pole	15°W, 60°N
30°	50°	60°E, 30°N	60°E, 80°N
30°	40°	South Pole	150°W, 60°S
50°	60°	45°E, 20°S	South Pole

7 The diagram shows the result of using three stars rather than two to navigate at sea.

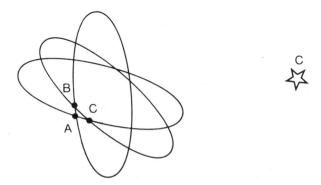

a Explain the advantages of using three stars rather than two.

b Where in △ ABC is it reasonable to assume the ship is?

---

*O*N YOUR OWN

Choose a point on a globe and imagine a star directly above. (You have chosen its GP.)

1   Spin the globe and observe what happens to the GP.

2   The GPs of all stars (except Polaris) change with time. Does the latitude of the GP change?

3   Find out how to read tables in a nautical almanac to get the GP of a star at a certain time. Does the use of nautical-almanac tables require an extremely accurate clock or *chronometer*? Explain why.

4   A number of important factors affect the accuracy of star navigation. Find out about these factors.

*O*N YOUR OWN

Navigators do not have globes on board ship on which to place latitude strings. Instead, they transfer their star fixes and other information onto special maps. Find out what these maps look like and how they are used.

CHECK-UP

1 A ship's navigator observes that on September 1 the sun is highest at 15:28 GMT. Find the ship's longitude at 15:28 GMT.

2 On the west coast, San Francisco is located at 37°N, 122°W, and Portland, Oregon, is at 45°N, 122°W.

   a What is the shortest route for an aircraft flying from San Francisco to Portland?

   b The circumference of the earth is about 25,000 miles. Calculate the minimum flying distance from San Francisco to Portland.

3 Use latitude strings and a globe to locate the positions on the earth indicated by the following information.

	Altitude	Geographical Position
First Star	60°	South Pole
Second Star	50°	30°S, 20°E

KEYMATH CONCEPTS

These KEYMATH activities can help you understand the math concepts you may need as you do the investigations. In the margins of the investigations, you sometimes see a little key. The number in the key identifies which KEYMATH activity you might want to review. Answers to the KEYMATH activities are given at the end of this section.

To round to a particular decimal place, look at the digit immediately to the right of that place. If it is 5 or larger, increase the rounded digit to the next higher value; if it is *less* than 5, do not change the rounded digit. Then drop any digits after the one you have rounded. For example, 2.467 rounded to the nearest tenth is 2.5.

Sometimes rounding is stated in terms of *significant digits*. A digit in a number is significant unless it is a zero whose only purpose is to help place the decimal point. That is, 0.05 has *one* significant digit (5) since the two zeros are included only to help place the decimal point properly; whereas 0.0600 has three significant digits (600). All non-zero digits in a number are significant. Thus, 435.62 has *five* significant digits. Zeros between two non-zero digits are also significant. Thus, 205.4 has *four* significant digits. Rounding 0.1448 to two significant digits gives you 0.15.

a Round 0.0800 to
   i   one decimal place.
   ii two significant digits.

b Round the numbers in the tables as indicated.

i

Number	Number of Decimal Places	Rounded Number
86.0908	1	
86.0908	2	
86.0908	3	
0.004906	3	
0.004906	4	
0.004906	5	

ii

Number	Number of Significant Figures	Rounded Number
174.0904	4	
174.0904	3	
174.0904	2	
0.06090	1	
0.06090	2	
0.06090	3	

2 When you are multiplying or dividing values that involve measures (length, weight, area, and so on), here's a good rule of thumb: Write the answer using *no more* significant digits than the *least* number of significant digits found in any of the numbers you used in the calculation. For example, it is sensible to write $3.5 \times 0.346 \approx 1.2$, since 3.5 has only two significant digits. (The symbol $\approx$ means *approximately equal to.*)

a Why is 8.900 m $\times$ 7.37 m $\approx$ 65.6 m^2 a sensible answer?

b Give sensible answers for the following:

i	10.9 m $\times$ 14.71 m		**vii**	291 km $\div$ 17 h
ii	16.88 km $\times$ 3.74 km		**viii**	381.4 km $\div$ 7.26 h
iii	188.8 cm^2 $\times$ 3.81 cm		**ix**	66.24 m^2 $\div$ 11.88 m
iv	10.8 km/h $\times$ 36.81 h		**x**	8804 cm^2 $\div$ 1.4 cm
v	0.0912 h/km $\times$ 14 km		**xi**	861.3 cm $\div$ 11.8 s
vi	808 cm $\times$ 414 cm		**xii**	441 m $\div$ 48.21 s

3 When you are multiplying or dividing three or more numbers, avoid rounding intermediate answers, because this generally leads to inaccurate answers.

a Show that $1.93 \times 6.36 \times 0.964 = 11.832\,907\,2$ (exactly).

b Show that $1.93 \times 6.36 \approx 12.3$ (rounded sensibly), and then $12.3 \times 0.964 = 11.857\,2$ (exactly).

c Explain why the two-step exercise in **b** gives an answer different from that in **a**, even though the same numbers are being multiplied.

d Repeat **a**, **b**, and **c** with a problem you make up yourself.

4 When you are solving problems that involve money, "sensible rounding" usually means rounding to the nearest cent or the nearest dollar. You generally would not use the significant-digit rounding rule, because you always want your answer to be in the form $XX or $XX.XX.

a Jenny pays $84.38 for 7 plates. Show that the cost of 1 plate is $12.05, rounded sensibly.

b Vince buys an 11-acre piece of property for $105 500. Show that an average cost of $9590 per acre is a sensibly rounded answer. Is $9600 a reasonable answer for some situations?

5

If $ax + b = c$, then $x = \dfrac{c - b}{a}$. If $a + bx = c$, then $x = \dfrac{c - a}{b}$

For example, if $5x + 4 = 15$, then $x = \dfrac{15 - 4}{5} = 2.2$

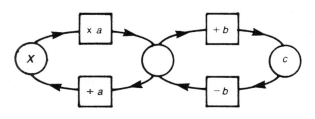

For $ax + b = c$

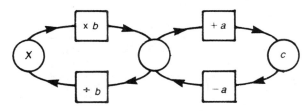

For $a + bx = c$

Solve the following. Use a calculator and round to three significant digits.

a $8.681x + 1.70 = 3.88$

b $181 + 8.9x = 199$

c $738 + 417x = 1089$

d $8.06x + 111 = 0$

e $17.48 - 8.81x = 0$

f $3.88x + 199 = 86.4$

6

a If $S = 4r^2$, use the flowchart or another method to explain why:

$r = \sqrt{\dfrac{S}{4}}$

b If $S = \pi r^3$, show that $r = \sqrt[3]{\dfrac{S}{\pi}}$

c Use the same pattern to find formulas for r in each of the following.

i $V = 4\pi r^3$

ii $S = 4\pi r^2$

iii $V = \dfrac{4\pi r^3}{3}$

iv $S = \dfrac{\pi r^2}{2}$

v $Z = \dfrac{3r^3}{8}$

vi $Z = \dfrac{\pi}{2} r^4$

For a car traveling a distance *d*, at average speed *s*, for a time *t*, then $d = s \times t$.

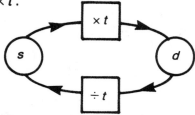 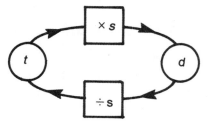

a Compute the missing values in the tables. (Round sensibly.)

i

d (ft)	t (s)	s (ft/s)
186	36	
334	11	
	20.6	12
40.5		20.1
	30.8	18.3

ii

d (mi)	t (h)	s (mph)
320.6	4.11	
480.8	8.07	
	4.0	40.66
300.4		100.62
	3.47	50.0

8

A car that consumes gasoline at a rate of *r* miles per gallon uses *g* gallons of gasoline. The distance *d* that it travels is found using the formula $d = g \times r$.

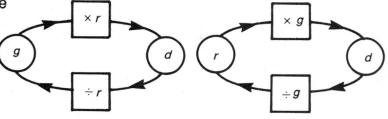

a A car travels 8061 miles. Its rate of gasoline consumption is 19.5 miles/gallon. Show that it uses about 413 gallons of gasoline for this trip.

b A car travels 2356 miles. Its rate of gasoline consumption is 32 miles/gallon. How many gallons of gasoline does the car use for this trip?

c Compute the missing values in the tables. (Round sensibly.)

i

d (mi)	g (gal)	r (mi/gal)
861	41.8	
76.8	3.6	
8688	339.3	
17408		29.6
	41.2	22.7

ii

d (mi)	g (gal)	r (mi/gal)
29681	1481	
	481.3	14.6
763.9		19.9
	81.7	24.5
	79.7	35.0

9

For a circle of radius r, diameter d, and circumference C,
$$C = 2\pi r = \pi d \quad \text{(where } \pi \approx 3.1415927\text{)}$$
$$d = 2r$$

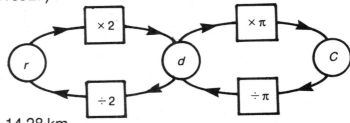

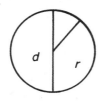

a If $C \approx 89.71$ km, show that $r \approx 14.28$ km.

b Compute the missing values in the tables. (Round sensibly. Refer to KEYMATH 2 for notes on rounding when measures are involved.)

i

r (km)	d (km)	C (km)
3.81		
4.68		
	12.48	
	3.019	
12.814		

ii

r (m)	d (m)	C (m)
	861	
		1482
		291.8
		1.190
		60.48

10

For a circle of radius r, diameter d, and area A, $A = \pi r^2$.

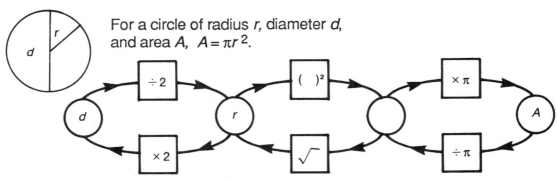

a If $A \approx 381$ cm^2, show that d ≈ 22.0 cm.

b Find the missing values in the tables. (Round sensibly.)

i

r (mm)	d (mm)	A (mm^2)
81		
40.9		
	126.6	
	300.4	

ii

r (cm)	d (cm)	A (cm^2)
		844
		89.91
		63.418
		4089

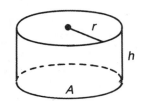

For a cylinder of volume V, radius r, height h, and cross-sectional area A,

$$V = Ah$$

or $$V = \pi r^2 h$$

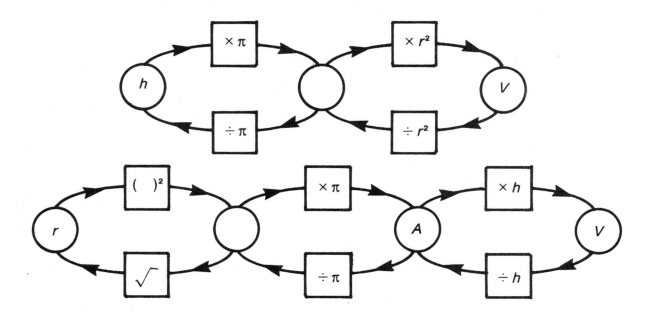

a **i** If $V \approx 375$ ml (375 cm³) and $r \approx 2.91$ cm, show that $h \approx 14.1$ cm is a sensible answer.

ii If $V \approx 451$ ml (451 cm³) and $h \approx 8.96$ cm, show that $r \approx 4.00$ cm is a sensible answer.

b Compute the missing values in the tables. (Round sensibly.)

i

h (mm)	r (mm)	V (mm³)
6.8	4.9	
34.8	21.3	
761	86.3	
	11.4	998.8

ii

h (cm)	r (cm)	V (cm³)
	19.6	2041
	24.6	2840
11.3		846.1
17.44		779.2

12

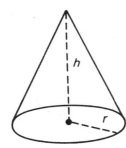

For a cone of radius r, height h, area of base A, and volume V,

$$V = \frac{1}{3} Ah = \frac{Ah}{3}$$

So $V = \frac{1}{3} \pi r^2 h = \frac{\pi r^2 h}{3}$

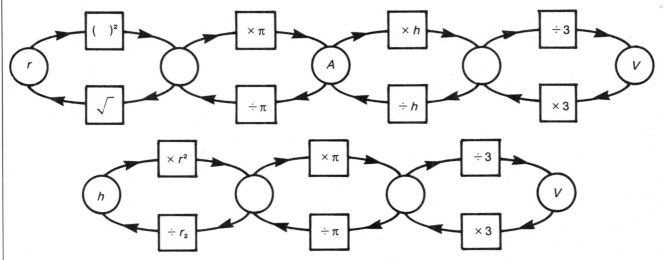

a If $V \approx 833$ cm³ and $h \approx 14.8$ cm, show that $r \approx 7.33$ cm is a sensible answer.

b Compute the missing values in the tables. (Round sensibly.)

i

h (cm)	r (cm)	V (cm³)
16.3	14.7	
28	13	
81.31	41.06	
	23.8	9014

ii

h (mm)	r (mm)	V (mm³)
	108.4	98143
61.4		8439
71.4		780639
22		777.8

13

To find 15% of a price P, you multiply the decimal/percent equivalent by the price in dollars and cents: $0.15 \times P$

Find the following percents. (Round sensibly.)

a 18% of $9.30

b 4.1% of $801

c 36% of $1440

d 86% of $11.37

e 6% of $3.91

f 14.8% of $41.41

14

a Percent means *per hundred*. To express a decimal number as a percent, multiply the decimal by 100 — or simply move the decimal point two places to the right. For example, 1.32 = 132%. Use a calculator to help explain why 16.3 ÷ 91.4 ≈ 0.178 = 17.8%.

b Use a calculator to do the following exercises, then express each decimal answer as a percent. (Round sensibly.)

i   17.8% ÷ 28.8 ≈ 0.___ = ___%   **v**   0.0481 ÷ 0.937 ≈ 0.___ = ___%

ii   86 ÷ 901 ≈ 0.___ = ___%   **vi**   381 ÷ 4884 ≈ 0.___ = ___%

iii   0.871 ÷ 0.978 ≈ 0.___ = ___%   **vii**   22 out of 35 ≈ 0.___ = ___%

iv   1.53 ÷ 39.87 ≈ 0.___ = ___%   **viii**   18 out of 29 ≈ 0.___ = ___%

15

Suppose you want to add on a certain percentage—say 15%—to a cost price *CP,* to find the selling price *SP.* This can be done in two ways.

Method A
$SP = (15\% \times CP) + CP$
$ = (0.15 \times CP) + CP$

Method B
$SP = 115\% \times CP$
$ = 1.15 \times CP$

The flowchart is based on Method B, for a markup of *r*%.

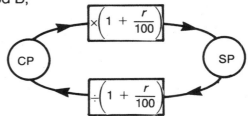

a A retailer marks up a radio by 35% and sells it for $319. Show that *CP* ≈ $236 is a sensible answer.

b Compute the missing values in the tables. (Round to the nearest dollar).

i

CP ($)	Markup	SP ($)
914	31%	
741	28%	
13406	81%	
	42%	41 231

ii

CP ($)	Markup	SP ($)
	70%	55
	21%	882
2811	−28%	
419		713

16

Suppose you want to subtract a certain percentage, say 18%, from a usual price UP to find the discount price DP. This can be done in two ways.

Method A
$$DP = UP - (18\% \times UP)$$
$$= UP - (0.18 \times UP)$$

Method B
$$DP = 82\% \times UP$$
$$= 0.82 \times UP$$

The flowchart is based on Method B, for a reduction of $r\%$.

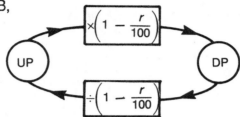

a A retailer discounts a $48 shirt by 30%. Show that $DP \approx \$34$ is a sensible answer.

b Compute the missing values in the tables. (Round to the nearest dollar.)

i

UP ($)	Discount	DP ($)
804	41%	
9141	7%	
487	19%	
	26%	3091

ii

UP ($)	Discount	DP ($)
	21%	788
	47%	10814
91	4%	
814	14%	

17

If a price increases first by $r_1\%$, then by another $r_2\%$, the total increase is *not* $(r_1 + r_2)\%$.

a A bicycle that used to cost $289.50 has increased in price by 8.3% Show that the new price is $313.53.

b The price of the bicycle in **a** is raised further by 17.6%. Show that the price is now $368.71.

c The sum of the two rate increases is 8.3% + 17.6% = 25.9%. Demonstrate that simply increasing the original price of $289.50 by 25.9% does not give the correct answer shown in **b**. Explain why.

d Repeat **a**, **b**, and **c** with a problem you make up yourself.

18

For a triangle of base b,
height h, and area A,
$$A = \frac{1}{2}bh$$

a If $A = 60 \text{ cm}^2$ and $h = 10$ cm, show that $b = 12$ cm.

b Compute the missing values in the tables. (Rounding is not required.)

i

b (mm)	h (mm)	A (mm²)
70	80	
100	60	
110	80	
140	100	

ii

b (cm)	h (cm)	A (cm²)
16		80
	20	100
40		200
	200	10000

19

For a rectangle of length x, width y,
area A, and perimeter P,
$$A = xy$$
$$P = 2(x + y) = 2x + 2y$$

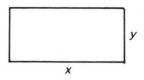

a If $A = 60 \text{ cm}^2$ and $x = 6$ cm, show that $P = 32$ cm.

b Compute the missing values in the tables. (Round to the nearest whole number.)

i

x (cm)	y (cm)	P (cm)	A (cm²)
6	8		
10	14		
8	12		
10			80
	8		160

ii

x (cm)	y (cm)	P (cm)	A (cm²)
4	5		
9			81
	7	26	
	10	34	
		22	30

20

For a cuboid with sides x, y, and z, total surface area T, and volume V:

area of front face = xy
area of side face = yz
area of bottom face = xz
$T = 2xy + 2yz + 2xz = 2(xy + yz + xz)$
$V = xyz$

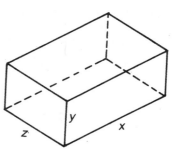

a If $x \approx 13.8$, $y \approx 14.9$ cm, $z \approx 20.8$ cm, show that $T \approx 1610$ cm^2 is a sensible answer.

b Compute the missing values in the table.

x (cm)	y (cm)	z (cm)	$2xy$ (cm^2)	$2yz$ (cm^2)	$2xz$ (cm^2)	T (cm^2)	V (cm^3)
18.4	20.31	24.6					
181.8	204.3	86.4					
8.44	9.38	23.86					
174	288	83.1					
1.093	2.143	2.880					
0.921	0.921	0.921					

c If $x \approx 12.8$ cm, $y \approx 15.3$ cm, and $T \approx 1584$ cm^2, find z.

d For a cube with side x, show that $T = 6x^2$.

21

Here are two ways to find the area of a polygonal figure. The method you choose in any given case may depend on the shape of the polygon.

Method A
Inscribe the polygon (E) in a rectangle. Find the area of each of the figures that surround the polygon (in the diagram, triangles A, B, C, and D). Add those areas and subtract the total from the area of the entire rectangle to find the area of polygon E.

Method B
Draw lines to divide the polygonal figure into triangular and rectangular shapes (in the diagram, triangles F, H, and I and rectangle G). Find the area of each of these smaller figures and total them to find the area of the entire polygon.

a Find the area of
   i A   **ii** B   **iii** C   **iv** D
   (See KEYMATH 18, if necessary, for notes on finding the area of a triangle.)

Method A   **Method B**

b Find the area of E using your answers in **a**.

c Use the second diagram and Method B to find the area of polygon E.

---

a If a batter scores n runs in x innings at an average of a runs per inning, explain why $n = ax$.

b i Kevin averages 0.68 runs per inning in 47 innings. What is his total number of runs?

ii The next season, Kevin averages 0.74 runs in 27 innings. What is his total number of runs this season?

iii Show that his average over the two seasons is 0.70.

c Compute the missing values in the table.

First Season			Second Season			Average Over Two Seasons
Runs	Innings Completed	Average	Runs	Innings Completed	Average	
	13	0.15		18	0.61	
	26	0.38		8	0.38	
	41	0.20	13		0.72	
5	12		8		0.53	

23

A car moves d feet in t seconds.

a Using the data in this chart, show that the car moves 5 feet in the third second and that its average speed at that point is 5 ft/s.

t	d
0	0
1	3
2	7
3	12
4	14
5	15

Start Time (s)	Finish Time (s)	Average Speed (ft/s)
0	5	
1	4	
2	4	
2	5	
3	5	
4	5	

b Show that the average speed in the fourth second is 2 ft/s.

c Show that the average speed from $t = 1$ to $t = 5$ is 3 ft/s.

d Use the data in the chart to compute the missing values in the table.

24

For a right triangle with sides *a*, *b*, and *c*,

$$a^2 = b^2 + c^2$$
$$b^2 = a^2 - c^2$$
$$c^2 = a^2 - b^2$$

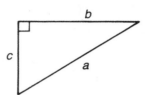

a If $a \approx 11.6$ cm and $b = 8.6$ cm, show that $c \approx 7.8$ cm.

b Compute the missing values in the tables. (Round to one decimal place.)

i

b (m)	*c* (m)	*a* (m)
14.9	12.6	
50.3	60.7	
1.7	3.8	
4.2		5.9
	3.9	6.9

ii

b (cm)	*c* (cm)	*a* (cm)
261.8	268.7	
	274.4	401.9
	407.9	581.3
281.8	384.7	
	46.9	46.0

25

Shown here is a rough sketch of △ABC. Use a compass and a ruler to make an accurate drawing of △ABC as described below.

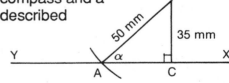

a Draw a line segment $\overline{YX}$.

b Construct a line segment $\overline{BC}$ 35 mm long at right angles to $\overline{YX}$.

c Set the compass for a radius of 50 mm and, using B as the center, make an arc at A. Draw line segment $\overline{AB}$.

d Show that the following are true by measuring with a ruler and protractor:
  i $\overline{AC} \approx 36$ mm
  ii $\alpha \approx 44°$

Repeat the steps above to draw five more triangles, using the values in the table.

$\overline{BC}$ (mm)	$\overline{AB}$ (mm)	$\overline{AC}$ (mm)	α
35	50	36	44°
25	70		
35	65		
41	49		
53	68		

26

The directions or bearings on a compass can be measured in degrees, starting with due north at 0° and proceeding clockwise.

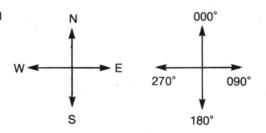

a Determine the missing facts in the tables.

i

Compass Point	Bearing
N	
NE	
E	
SE	

ii

Compass Point	Bearing
	180°
	225°
	270°
	315°

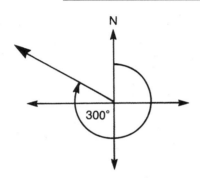

b This diagram shows a bearing of about 300°. Without using a protractor, draw bearings of:

i	080°	**v**	350°
ii	240°	**vi**	210°
iii	195°	**vii**	020°
iv	100°	**viii**	295°

27

When no parentheses are indicated in a series of computations, carry out the operations in the following order:

- First calculate × and ÷ from left to right.
- Then calculate + and − from left to right.

a Show that $^-3 \times {}^-2 - {}^-5 \times 2 = 16$.

b Compute the following.

i	$^-2 \times {}^-3 \times {}^-1 =$ ___	**v**	$^-1 \times 6 - {}^-2 \times {}^-3 =$ ___
ii	$6 - {}^-2 \times {}^-4 =$ ___	**vi**	$^-2 \times {}^-2 \times 2 \times {}^-2 - {}^-8 =$ ___
iii	$^-3 \times {}^-4 - {}^-14 =$ ___	**vii**	$26 - {}^-4 \times {}^-4 =$ ___
iv	$1 \times 2 - 2 \times 4 + 4 \times {}^-1 =$ ___	**viii**	$^-1 \times 3 - 1 \times 3 - {}^-1 \times 8 =$ ___

28

In the expression 3^4, the value 3 is called the *base* and 4 is called the *exponent.* The expression $3^4 = 3 \times 3 \times 3 \times 3 = 81$.

Complete the following equations.

a $16 = 2^{\square}$

b $8 = 2^{\square}$

c $4 = 2^{\square}$

d $2 = 2^{\square}$

e $1 = 2^{\square}$

f $2^6 = \underline{\hspace{1cm}}$

g $2^8 = \underline{\hspace{1cm}}$

h $3^4 = \underline{\hspace{1cm}}$

i $10^3 = \underline{\hspace{1cm}}$

j $5^3 = \underline{\hspace{1cm}}$

k $8^2 = \underline{\hspace{1cm}}$

l $8^0 = \underline{\hspace{1cm}}$

29

The following are examples of the *distributive* property of multiplication over addition and multiplication over subtraction:

$$a(b+c) = ab + ac$$
and $$(a+b)c = ac + bc$$

$$a(b-c) = ab - ac$$
and $$(a-b)c = ac - bc$$

a Explain why $2x(3x - 4) = 6x^2 - 8x$.

b Expand each of the following expressions.

i $3x(4x + 3) =$

ii $2x(1 - 2x) =$

iii $x(3 - 4x) =$

iv $(3y + 1)y =$

v $(4y + 3)y =$

vi $2y(7 - 3y) =$

vii $(y + 7)y =$

viii $(3f - 1)f =$

30

If two equations have one variable in common, it is generally possible to reduce the two expressions to a single equation by substitution.

a If $z = xy$ and $y = 2x^2$, explain why $z = 2x^3$. (Note that the y has been eliminated.)

b Reduce each of the following pairs to a single equation by eliminating the y variable.

i $z = yx^2$ and $y = 3x$

ii $z = y^2x$ and $y = x$

iii $z = y^2x^2$ and $y = 2x$

iv $y = 4r$ and $z = 2r^2y^2$

v $y = \frac{1}{2}x$ and $z = 8x^2y$

vi $y = \frac{x}{2}$ and $z = 8xy^2$

31

When you have a two-column table, you can often find a general rule, or *formula,* that relates all pairs of values in the table. Information that is provided in the problem statement may help you discover the formula.

a Jill orders x shirts at \$15 each from a mail order house. Postage and handling is \$4 for any order. She pays a total of C. Complete this table relating the number and cost of shirts.

x	C ($\$$)	*Pattern*
1	19	
2	34	$(2 \times 15) + 4$
3		
4		
5		

b Determine the formula for this table. (*Hint:* $C = \square\, x + \Delta$)

c Find a formula for each of the following tables.

i

x	C
1	5
2	9
3	13
4	17

ii

x	C
1	7
2	10
3	13
4	16

iii

x	C
1	9
2	14
3	19
4	24

32

If you buy three times as much of something, you would generally expect to pay three times the price. For example, suppose 2 loaves of bread cost $1.50. To buy 6 loaves, you would have to spend 3 times as much, or $4.50.

The ratio of the new amount (6) to the old amount (2) is $\frac{6}{2} = 3$. We call this number the *scale factor.* We can use it to determine cost.

a Jack pays $12.50 for a 1.65 m length of material. Joan buys 2.85 m of the same material and wants to know its cost.

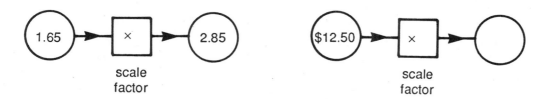

Use a calculator to show that the number missing from the scale factor box in the flowchart must be 1.727 272 7.

b Use **a** to show that Joan will pay $21.59 for her material.

c Use a calculator to compute the missing values in the following table.

Length of Material A (m)	Cost of Length A ($)	Length of Material B (m)	Scale Factor (unrounded)	Cost of Length B ($)
1.65	12.50	2.85	1.727 272 7	21.59
3.50	36.40	5.50		
4.25	89.20	26.50		
12.50	114.50	14.50		
3.75	36.75	2.25		
7.50	91.25	3.50		

33 Equations of the form $x = ay + b$ have several pairs of numbers (x,y) that make the equation true. If you graph these pairs of (x,y) values as points on a coordinate plane, their graph will be a straight line. For example, consider the following points for the equation $x = 3y - 1$:

$$(2, 1) \rightarrow 2 = 3 \times 1 - 1$$
$$(5, 2) \rightarrow 5 = 3 \times 2 - 1$$
$$(8, 3) \rightarrow 8 = 3 \times 3 - 1$$

FIll in the numbers that make the following equations true.

a $y = 2x + 1$ $(1, 3), (2, \underline{}), (3, \underline{}), (6, \underline{})$

b $x = 3y - 4$ $(5, 3), (\underline{}, 2), (\underline{}, 0), (\underline{}, 5)$

c $y = 2x - 1$ $(3, \underline{}), (2, \underline{}), (\underline{}, 7), (\underline{}, 9)$

d $x + y = 7$ $(1, 6), (4, \underline{}), (\underline{}, 4), (\underline{}, 0)$

e $2x + 3y = 18$ $(0, \underline{}), (3, \underline{}), (\underline{}, 6), (\underline{}, 2)$

f $5x + 3y = 45$ $(0, \underline{}), (3, \underline{}), (6, \underline{}), (\underline{}, 15)$

34 The graph of an inequality of the form $ax + by \leq c$ or $ax + by \geq c$ fills half of the coordinate plane. To construct a graph of the inequality $x + y \leq 6$, we first graph the equality $x + y = 6$, then determine on which side of the line are the points that make the inequality true. In this example, the graph of $x + y \leq 6$ is shaded below the line because a point like $(0, 0)$ or $(1, 1)$ satisfies the inequality.

Note that the graph for any $\leq$ and $\geq$ inequality *includes the points on the line,* whereas the graph for any $<$ or $>$ inequality does *not* include the points on the line. For graphs of the latter type, use a dotted line to indicate that the line is not included in the graph, as shown in the second example.

Draw graphs of the following inequalities.

a $x + y < 6$

b $x + y \geq 6$

c $x - y \leq 8$

d $y > 2x - 4$

e $y \leq 2x - 4$

f $3x + 7y \leq 21$

g $x > 2y + 1$

h $3y + 2x \geq 12$

i $y - 2x \geq 8$

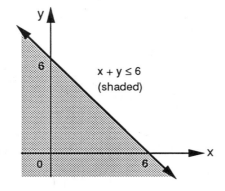

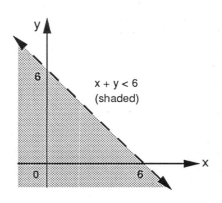

Figure A has *rotational symmetry* because we can rotate the rectangle less than a full turn about a point in the center square to a second position that exactly matches its starting position. Figure B has *line symmetry* because we can draw a vertical line through the center squares, and the rectangle, when flipped across that line, exactly matches its starting position.

Figure A

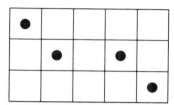

Figure B

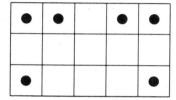

Make two copies of each of the following four figures. Add additional dots to each figure to give them the following properties:

   i rotational but *not* line symmetry.
   ii line but *not* rotational symmetry.

a

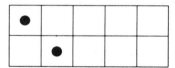

b

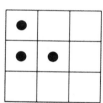

c

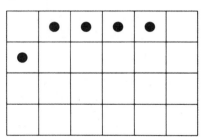

d

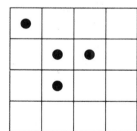

KEY MATH CONCEPTS

Answers

1 **a i** 0.1
  a ii 0.080
  b i 86.1, 86.09, 86.091, 0.005, 0.004 9, 0.004 91
  b ii 174.1, 174, 170, 0.06, 0.061, 0.0609

2 **a** The number 8.900 has 4 significant figures and 7.37 has 3 significant figures. The product should have 3 significant figures.
  b i 160 m^2
  b ii 63.1 km^2
  b iii 719 cm^3
  b iv 398 km
  b v 1.3 h
  b vi 335 000 cm^2
  b vii 17 km/h
  b viii 52.5 km/h
  b ix 5.576 m
  b x 6 300 cm
  b xi 73.0 cm/s
  b xii 9.15 m/s

3 **c** The rounding in **b** was done too early.

4 **a** $84.38 ÷ 7 = $12.054285, or $12.05
  b Yes, when an approximate cost to the nearest $100 is sufficient.

5 **a** 0.251
  b 2.02
  c 0.842
  d −13.7
  e 1.98
  f −29.0

6 **c i** $r = \sqrt[3]{\dfrac{V}{4\pi}}$ **c ii** $r = \sqrt{\dfrac{S}{4\pi}}$

  c iii $r = \sqrt[3]{\dfrac{3V}{4\pi}}$ **c iv** $r = \sqrt{\dfrac{2S}{\pi}}$

  c v $r = \sqrt[3]{\dfrac{8Z}{3}}$ **c vi** $r = \sqrt[4]{\dfrac{2Z}{\pi}}$

7 **a i**

d (ft)	t (s)	s (ft/s)
186	36	**5.2**
334	11	**30**
250	20.6	12
40.5	**2.01**	20.1
564	30.8	18.3

a ii

d (mi)	t (h)	s (mph)
320.6	4.11	**78.0**
480.8	8.07	**59.6**
160	4.0	40.66
300.4	**2.985**	100.62
174	3.47	50.0

8 **a** 8061 ÷ 19.5 = 413.38, or about 413 gallons.
  b About 74 gallons.
  c i

d (mi)	g (gal)	r (mi/gal)
861	41.8	**20.6**
76.8	3.6	**21.3**
8688	339.3	**25.6**
17408	**588.1**	29.6
935	41.2	22.7

  c ii

d (mi)	g (gal)	r (mi/gal)
29681	1481	**20.0**
7027	481.3	14.6
763.9	**38.4**	19.9
2002	81.7	24.5
2789.5	79.7	35.0

9 **a** r = 89.71 ÷ 2 (3.1416) = 14.277756, or 14.28 (2 significant places)
  b i

r (km)	d (km)	C (km)
3.81	**7.62**	**23.9**
4.68	**9.36**	**29.4**
6.24	12.48	**39.21**
1.510	3.019	**9.484**
12.814	25.628	**80.513**

  b ii

r (m)	d (m)	C (m)
431	861	**2700**
235.9	**471.7**	1482
46.44	92.88	291.8
0.1894	**0.3788**	1.190
9.626	**19.25**	60.48

10 a $r = \sqrt{\dfrac{381}{\pi}} = 11.0$, so $d = 22.0$

b i

r (mm)	d (mm)	A (mm^2)
81	**162**	**21000**
40.9	**81.8**	**5260**
63.3	126.6	**12590**
150.2	300.4	**70870**

b ii

r (cm)	d (cm)	A (cm^2)
16.4	**32.8**	844
5.350	**10.70**	89.91
4.4929	**8.9859**	63.418
36.08	**72.15**	4089

11 a i $h = \dfrac{375}{2.91^2} \div \pi \approx 14.1$ cm

a ii $r = \sqrt{\dfrac{451}{8.96} \div \pi} \approx 4.00$ cm

b i

h (mm)	r (mm)	V (mm^3)
6.8	4.9	**510**
34.8	21.3	**49600**
761	86.3	**17800000**
2.45	11.4	998.8

b ii

h (cm)	r (cm)	V (cm^3)
1.69	19.6	2041
1.49	24.6	2840
11.3	**4.88**	846.1
17.44	**3.771**	779.2

12 a i $r = \sqrt{\dfrac{833 \times 3}{14.8} \div \pi} \approx 7.33$ cm

b i

h (cm)	r (cm)	V (cm^3)
16.3	14.7	**3690**
28	13	**5000**
81.31	41.06	**143600**
15.2	23.8	9014

b ii

h (mm)	r (mm)	V (mm^3)
7.976	108.4	98143
61.4	**11.5**	8439
71.4	**102**	780639
22	**5.8**	777.8

13 a $1.67
b $33
c $518
d $9.78

e $ .23
f $6.13

14 b i 0.618 = 61.8%
b ii 0.095 = 9.5%
b iii 0.891 = 89.1%
b iv 0.0384 = 3.84%
b v 0.0513 = 5.13%
b vi 0.0780 = 7.80%
b vii 0.63 = 63%
b viii 0.62 = 62%

15 a By Method B: $319 ÷ 1.35 = about $236

b i

CP ($)	Markup	SP ($)
914	31%	**1197**
741	28%	**948**
13406	81%	**24265**
29036	42%	41231

b ii

CP ($)	Markup	SP ($)
32	70%	55
729	21%	882
2811	–28%	**2024**
419	**70%**	713

16 a Method B: $48 × 0.70 = 33.6 or about $34

b i

UP ($)	Discount	DP ($)
804	41%	**474**
9141	7%	**8501**
487	19%	**394**
4177	26%	3091

b ii

UP ($)	Discount	DP ($)
997	21%	788
20404	47%	10814
91	4%	**87**
814	14%	**700**

17 a Price = $298.50 × 1.083 ≈ $313.53
b Price = $298.50 × 1.083 x 1.176 ≈ $368.71
c $289.50 × 1.259 ≈ $364.48 ≠ $368.71 from **b**.

18 a $\dfrac{2A}{h} = b$, so $120 \div 10 = 12$
b i A (mm^2): 2 800, 3 000, 4 400, 7 000
b ii

b (cm)	h (cm)	A (cm^2)
16	**10**	80
10	20	100
40	**10**	200
100	200	10000

19 a $y = 10$ cm, $P = 2 \times 10 + 2 \times 6 = 32$ cm

b i

x (cm)	y (cm)	P (cm)	A (cm^2)
6	8	**28**	**48**
10	14	**48**	**140**
8	12	**40**	**96**
10	8	**36**	80
20	8	**56**	160

b ii

x (cm)	y (cm)	P (cm)	A (cm^2)
4	5	**18**	**20**
9	9	**36**	81
6	7	26	**42**
7	10	34	**70**
6 or 5	**5 or 6**	22	30

20 a T = $(2 \times 13.8 \times 14.9) + (2 \times 14.9 \times 20.8) + (2 \times 13 \times 20.8) \approx 1610$ cm^2 (3 sig figs)

b

$2xy$ (cm^2)	$2yz$ (cm^2)	$2xz$ (cm^2)
747.408	**999.252**	**905.28**
74283.48	**35303.04**	**31415.04**
1583344	**447.6136**	**402.7568**
100224	**47865.6**	**28918.8**
4.684598	**12.34368**	**6.29568**
1.696482	**1.696482**	**1.696482**

T (cm^2)	V (cm^3)
2650	**9190**
141000	**3210000**
1010	**1890**
177000	**4160000**
23.32	**6.746**
5.09	**0.781**

c 21.2 cm

d $x = y = z$. So T = $2x^2 + 2x^2 + 2x^2 = 6x^2$

21 a i 2 units^2

a ii 3 units^2

a iii 3 units^2

a iv 3 units^2

b 14 units^2

c F = 5 units^2; G = 3 units^2; H = 3 units^2; I = 3 units^2; so E = 14 units^2

22 a If there are a runs in each inning and altogether there x innings, then there are ax runs scored. So $n = ax$.

b i 32 runs

b ii 20 runs

c

First Season		
Runs	Innings Completed	Average
2	13	0.15
10	26	0.38
8	41	0.20
5	12	**0.42**

Second Season			Average Over Two Seasons
Runs	Innings Completed	Average	
11	18	0.61	**0.42**
3	8	0.38	**0.38**
13	**18**	0.72	**0.36**
8	**15**	0.53	**0.48**

23 a Average speed = $\dfrac{12 - 7}{3 - 2}$ = 5 ft/s

b Average speed = $\dfrac{14 - 12}{4 - 3}$ = 2 ft/s

c Average speed = $\dfrac{15 - 3}{5 - 1}$ = 3 ft/s

d Average speed (ft/s): 3, $3\frac{2}{3}$, $3\frac{1}{2}$, $2\frac{2}{3}$, $1\frac{1}{2}$, 1

24 a $c^2 = (11.6)^2 - (8.6)^2 = 60.6$, so $c \approx 7.8$

b i

b (m)	c (m)	a (m)
14.9	12.6	**19.5**
50.3	60.7	**78.8**
1.7	3.8	**4.2**
4.2	**4.1**	5.9
5.7	3.9	6.9

b ii

b (cm)	c (cm)	a (cm)
261.8	268.7	**375.2**
293.6	274.4	401.9
414.2	407.9	581.3
281.8	384.7	**476.9**
impossible	46.9	46.0

25

BC (mm)	AB (mm)	AC (mm)	α
35	50	36	44°
25	70	**65**	**21°**
35	65	**55**	**33°**
41	49	**27**	**57°**
53	68	**43**	**51°**

26 a i Bearing: 000°, 045°, 090°, 135°

a ii Compass point: S, SW, W, NW

b i

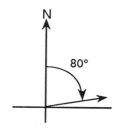

80°

b ii

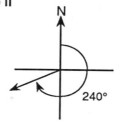

240°

b iii

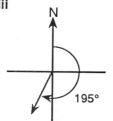

195°

b iv

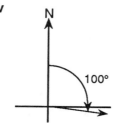

100°

b v

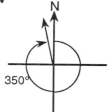

350°

b vi

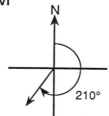

210°

b vii

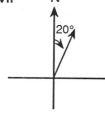

20°

b viii

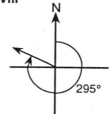

295°

27 a $(-3 \times -2) - (-5 \times 2) = 6 - (-10) = 16$
b i –6
b ii –2
b iii 2
b iv –10
b v 0
b vi –8
b vii 10
b viii 2

28 a 2^4
b 2^3
c 2^2
d 2^1
e 2^0
f 64
g 256
h 81
i 1000
j 125
k 64
l 1

29 a $2x(3x-4) = 2x \times 3x - 2x \times 4 = 6x^2 - 8x$
b i $12x^2 + 9x$
b ii $2x - 4x^2$
b iii $3x - 4x^2$
b iv $3y^2 + y$
b v $4y^2 + 3y$
b vi $14y - 6y^2$
b vii $y^2 + 7y$
b viii $3f^2 - f$

30 a $z = xy = x \times 2x^2 = 2x^3$
b i $z = 3x^3$
b ii $z = x^3$
b iii $z = 4x^4$
b iv $z = 32r^4$
b v $z = 4x^3$
b vi $z = 2x^3$

31 a

x	C (\$)	Pattern
1	19	$(1 \times 15) + 4$
2	34	$(2 \times 15) + 4$
3	49	$(3 \times 15) + 4$
4	64	$(4 \times 15) + 4$
5	79	$(5 \times 15) + 4$

b $C = 15x + 4$
c i $C = 4x + 1$
c ii $C = 3x + 4$
c iii $C = 5x + 4$

32 b $\$12.50 \times 1.727\,272\,7 = \$21.59$
c

Scale Factor (unrounded)	Cost of Length B (\$)
1.7272727	21.59
1.5714286	57.20
6.2352941	556.19
1.16	132.82
0.6	22.05
0.4666667	42.58

33 a (1,3), (2,5), (3,7), (6,13)
b (5,3), (2,2), (–4,0), (11,5)
c (3,5), (2,3), (4,7), (5,9)
d (1,6), (4,3), (3,4), (7,0)
e (0,6), (3,4), (0,6), (6,2)
f (0,15), (3,10), (6,5), (0,15)

34
a

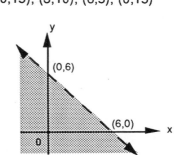

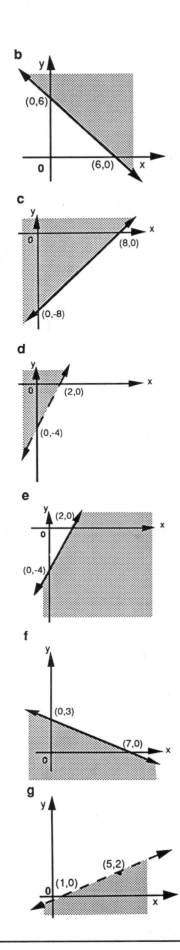

b

(0,6)

(6,0) x

0

c

0 y x

(8,0)

(0,-8)

d

0 y x

(2,0)

(0,-4)

e

(2,0) y x

0

(0,-4)

f

(0,3)

(7,0) x

0

g

y

(5,2)

0 (1,0)

x

h

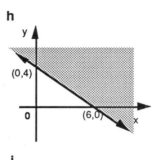

y

(0,4)

0

(6,0) x

i

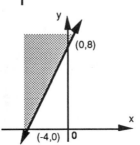

y

(0,8)

x

(-4,0) 0

35 There are many possible answers. For example:

a i **a ii**

b i 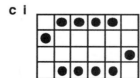 **b ii**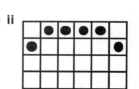

c i 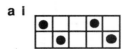 **c ii**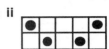

d i Not possible, as rotations always produce line symmetry, also.

d ii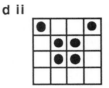

MATHEMATICAL INVESTIGATIONS · DALE SEYMOUR PUBLICATIONS

INVESTIGATIONS

Answer Key

Note: Oversized tables and figures for the Answer key are grouped at the end, starting on page 220.

CHAPTER 1   NETWORKS

Investigation One —
The Mailcarrier Problem

1 No

2 No

3 **a** An odd vertex has an odd number of roads connecting it to other vertices, and an even vertex has an even number of connecting roads.
b Networks ii, iii, vi, vii, and ix have solutions.
c [Table 1.1–see page 220]
d If a network has no odd vertices, there is always a solution.

4 **a** One route for Lisa is: X to A to B to C to D to Y to E to F to G to H to D to J to G to I to K to J to B to L to K to M to X.
b Yes, there are many possible solutions.
c Since there are no odd vertices, there is a solution for any starting point.

5 A and B are both odd vertices but can be made into "even" vertices by traveling AB twice.

On Your Own   **Page 6**

Consider whether it is optimal to deliver mail by zigzagging from one side of a road to the other or whether the quickest route is along one side of the road and then back along the other side.

---

6 **a** Yes, because the new network has no odd vertices.
b A and B can be made even by traveling the road AB twice.

7 Odd vertices should be made even by adding new roads (dotted). Each network can then be traveled in many ways.

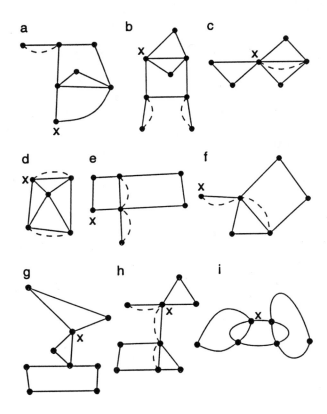

On Your Own   **Page 8**

Many designers of pathways do not plan exact locations without first taking into account the well-worn routes made by people. These routes are invariably easier to use than landscape-designed routes. If there are no people-made routes for designers to make use of, temporary pathways are sometimes provided that can be easily altered to take into account people-made routes later. Rutgers University reportedly designed its walkways using this technique.

---

1 a

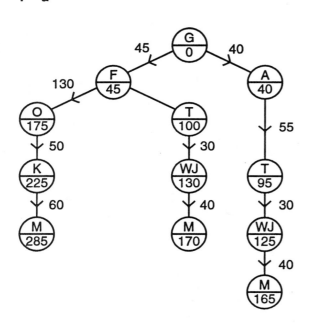

b 2 hours and 45 minutes (Geralville via Aarron)
c 4 hours and 25 minutes

2 a

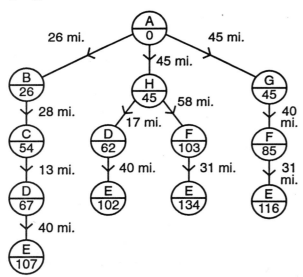

b A to H to D to E (102 miles)

3 a

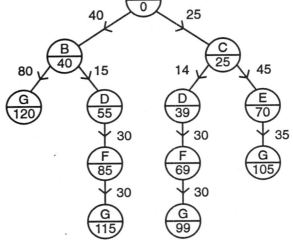

b A to C to D to F to G (99 units)
c A to C to E to G (105 units)

4 a A to B to D to C to H (1 040 meters)
b A to B to D to E to G to J to H (1 200 meters)

5 a A to B to E to F (72 miles)
b A to B to C to F (2.22 hours, or 2 hours, 13 minutes, and 12 seconds)

6 a–b The two shortest routes (of equal length) are shown.

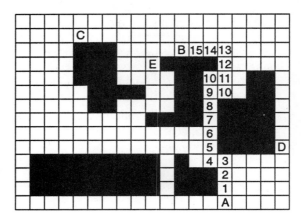

7 a

b Many routes are possible. Four of the shortest are shown.

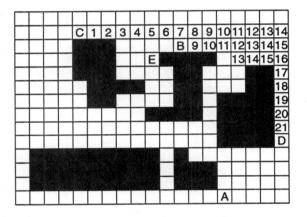

c Many routes are possible. Several of the shortest are shown.

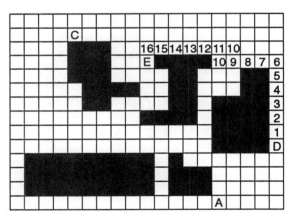

d Two of the possible shortest routes are shown.

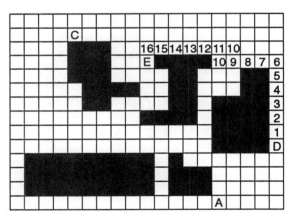

8 **a** Home to B to C to F to Work (27 time units)
   b i Home to B to C to F to Work (33.5 time units)
   ii Home to B to C to F to Work (25.6 time units)
   iii Home to B to G to F to Work (31 time units)

Investigation Three — Connected Networks

1 **a** BE is the longest pipe, and its removal still leaves the sprinklers connected.
   b This will disconnect B from the network.
   c Yes
   d Remove from the original diagram in the following order: BE, then DE, then AC.
   e Yes
   f The total length of Jan's design is 175 units, while Jerry's is 194 units.
   g No connected network is shorter than Jan's.
2 Remove the longest remaining segments, unless this disconnects the points from the network paths to AB, BC, CD, DE, and DF. The shortest (cheapest) network is therefore AB, BC, CD, DE, and DF.
3 The sides and minimum lengths are:
   a AD, DG, GE, EB, BC, CF (48 units)
   b AB, AE, EF, FD, FC (39 units)
   c AI, IJ, IG, GF, FH, FE, EC, CD, CB (81 units)
   d AE, EC, EB, BG, GD, DF (240 units)

4 **a i**

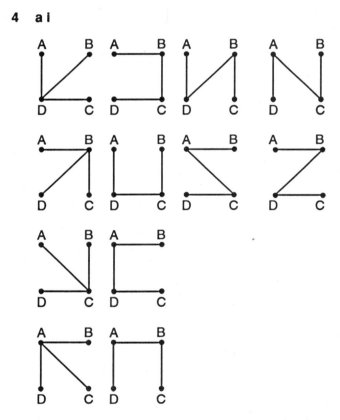

ii All cases require exactly three line segments.

b Examples are: (i)

(ii)

(iii)

c

p	n
2	1
3	2
4	3
5	4
20	19
81	80

d i It is always possible to connect six points with five line segments.

ii

e i A seven-point network requires six line segments, so a seven-point network with five line segments has a point that is disconnected.

ii

5 In such problems, there should always be one fewer line segments than points.

On Your Own   **Page 17**

Jan's rules always work.

6 AY, YB, AD, DX, XC or AY, YB, BC, DX, XC.
7 $8,150,000

8 The shortest connected network is Kittery, Portland, Brunswick, Augusta, Waterville, Bangor, Ellsworth, Eastport, Houlton, and Van Buren; Brunswick and Bath; Brunswick and Lewiston; Ellsworth, Belfast, and Rockland; Ellsworth and Bar Harbor; Ellsworth, Eastport, Houlton, and Van Buren (517 miles).

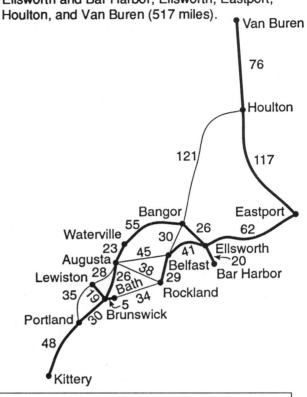

On Your Own   **Page 19**

The shortest connected network is Los Angeles, San Francisco, and Seattle; Los Angeles and Las Vegas; Los Angeles, San Diego, Phoenix, Tucson, El Paso, Dallas, Houston, and New Orleans; Phoenix, Albuquerque, and Denver; Dallas, Oklahoma City, Kansas City, Memphis, Nashville, and Atlanta; Nashville, Cincinnati, and Chicago; Cincinnati, Pittsburgh, Philadelphia, Washington D. C., Baltimore, New York, Albany, and Boston; Pittsburgh, Cleveland, and Buffalo (8,128 miles).

[Fig 1–see page 220]

9 a

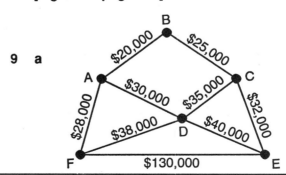

b i AF, AD, AB, BC, CE
  ii $135,000
10 Build AE, AD, AB, and BC.

CHAPTER ONE — Check-Up

1   a X to D to B to Y
    b Go over AB and EY twice each.
    c XD, DA, AB, BC, CY, and YE
2   a X to D to E to Y
    b Go over BY and AX twice each.
    c BE, EY, ED, DC, DX, and XA
3   a X to C to D to Y
    b No repeat journey is required.
    c DY, DE, EA, EB, BX, and XC
4   a X to F to C to Y
    b Go over FC and AB twice each.
    c AX, AB, BC, CE, EF, ED, and DY

CHAPTER 2   SPORTS MATH

Investigation One — Tournaments

1   a In round 2, C is supposed to play both A and B—which is impossible.
    b i The diagonal marked by × represents A vs. A and B vs. B—or a team playing itself, which makes no sense.
    ii

v	A	B	C
A	x	1	2
B	1	x	3
C	2	3	x

    iii In round 3, Team B plays Team C. In round 1, Team C doesn't play. In the words of a tournament master, it is assigned a *bye.*
    c i

v	A	B	C	D
A	x	1	2	3
B	1	x	3	2
C	2	3	x	1
D	3	2	1	x

    ii Yes, since the pattern of round numbers matches on either side of the diagonal of ×'s.
    d i As in problem c ii, A vs. B = B vs. A, B vs. C = C vs. B, and so on. The table is symmetrical about the main diagonal marked by ×'s.
    ii [Table 2.3–see page 221]
    iii [Table 2.4–see page 221]

e i Draw for eight teams:
  [Table 2.5–see page 221]
  ii Draw for ten teams
  [Table 2.6–see page 221]
2   a In problem 1 e i, create an eighth team "H" as a *bye* team. Any team that plays "H" is also assigned a bye for that round. So byes occur for each team in the following rounds: A in 7, B in 2, C in 4, D in 6, E in 1, F in 3, G in 5. (You can use the eight-team draw for e i as a reference.)
    b Make a draw for the odd number of teams plus 1. Any team due to play the extra team is then assigned a bye in that round—meaning that team won't play.
3   a

v	A	B
A	x	1
B	1	x

Number of games played: 1

v	A	B	C
A	x	1	2
B	1	x	3
C	2	3	x

Number of games played: 3

v	A	B	C	D
A	x	1	2	3
B	1	x	3	2
C	2	3	x	1
D	3	2	1	x

Number of games played: 6

    b Eleven teams play $\frac{11 \times 10}{2}$ games in all—or 55 games.
    c

Number of Games Played by Each Team	Total Number of Games Played
1	1
2	3
3	6
4	10
10	55

d The rule is $\frac{n(n-1)}{2}$ games for n teams. Each of the teams plays $n-1$ other teams, so there are apparently $n(n-1)$ games. However, A vs. B = B vs. A, and so on. If each of the games is counted twice in the total of $n(n-1)$, there are really only $\frac{n(n-1)}{2}$ games. Therefore, if there are n teams, there are $\frac{n(n-1)}{2}$ games.

e i When one side wins, that side gets 4 points and the loser 1 point. If the teams are tied, they each get 2 points (4 total). Therefore, at least 4 points are awarded every game. In an 11-team basketball league, there are 55 games—so at least 220 points (4×55) are awarded.
ii 11 games

f i $\frac{21 \times 20}{2} = 210$ games in the first round.

ii $21 \times 20 = 420$ games in total.

g $n(n-1)$ games

4 a France

b

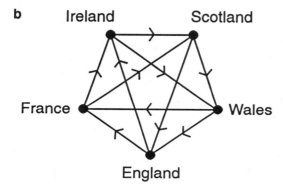

In this diagram, each team has two wins. (There are several ways to draw this diagram, depending on which nation beat which.)

c

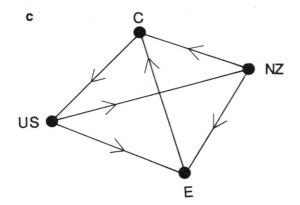

d i There are 6 games in all with 2 points for each game, so 12 points are awarded.
ii If the 4 teams were tied at the end of the tournament, they would share equally the 12 points—which means they would have to be awarded 3 points each. However, points are awarded only for wins (in multiples of 2), so teams cannot earn an odd number of points.

e i 42 points in all
ii Yes, if each team wins 3 games and therefore earns 6 points.

f i 56 points. However, all 8 teams cannot tie for first place in the competition; this would mean each team gets 7 points, which is impossible.
ii 72 points. All 9 teams can share the championship by each winning 4 games (or 8 points).
iii $n(n-1)$ points. All n (odd) teams can share the championship because $\frac{n(n-1)}{n} = n-1$ (an even number of points when n is odd).
iv $n(n-1)$ points. All n (even) teams cannot share the championship, because $\frac{n(n-1)}{n} = n-1$ (an odd number of points when n is even).

On Your Own   **Page 31**

In most sports played in in the United States and Canada, a tie at the end of regular time means the game goes into overtime until one side wins. When the United States started a soccer league, extra time was played in this way. However, in the rest of the world, ties are common. Overtime is not played unless the game is part of an elimination competition.

---

5 a An elimination competition with 2 players always produces 1 loser. A competition with 3 players produces 2 losers. For 10 players, there are 9 losers, and for 32 players there are 31 losers—which means 31 games must be played.
b An elimination competition with n players produces $(n-1)$ losers, which means $(n-1)$ games.
c The 56 players still produce 55 losers, which result from 55 games. The seeding only allows the top players to avoid elimination during round 1.
d The maximum number of games needed for a 5-player double elimination is $10 - 1 = 9$. (If it were a single-elimination tournament, the maximum number of games would be $5 - 1$, or

---

4.) Note that simply doubling the number of games for a single-elimination doesn't necessarily come up with the number of games in a double-elimination tournament. However, if one player goes undefeated, 8 games would be sufficient to find the winner. In general, for n players a maximum of $2n - 1$ games are needed in a double-elimination tournament.

On Your Own   **Page 33**

The 15 teams would need to play 14 games to find 14 losing teams and the winning team. The reason the organizers had Division C teams play first is they *seeded* the teams in Divisions A and B. They seeded these teams because the players in them were drawn from a larger pool of students and therefore were probably more competitive.

---

6 Each of the 6 groups plays 6 games in the round robins, or 36 games in all. The final 16 teams in Stage 2 need 15 games to find the winner. So the World Cup competition requires 36 + 15 = 51 games.

7 **a** The round-robin stage requires 4 groups of players × 6 games, or 24 games. The elimination stage involves 8 chess masters and requires 7 games during the elimination series. Altogether, 24 + 7 = 31 games are needed to find a champion.
   b Total attendance = 31 × 650 = 20,150

Investigation Two — Systematic Counting

1 **a** A touchdown is needed before a point-after (which is 1 point) can be attempted.
   b Just 1
   c Before 2 points-after can be scored, at least 2 touchdowns are needed. So 8 points from a single touchdown and 2 points-after is not possible.
   d

T	F	S	P	Total
2	0	0	0	12
1	2	0	0	12
1	1	1	1	12
1	0	3	0	12
0	4	0	0	12
0	2	3	0	12
0	0	6	0	12

2 **a**

T	F	S	P	Total
3	0	0	0	18
2	2	0	0	18
2	1	1	1	18
2	0	2	2	18
2	0	3	0	18
1	4	0	0	18
1	3	1	1	18
1	2	3	0	18
1	1	4	1	18
1	0	6	0	18
0	6	0	0	18
0	4	3	0	18
0	2	6	0	18
0	0	9	0	18

b

T	F	S	P	Total
3	0	0	1	19
2	2	0	1	19
2	1	1	2	19
2	0	3	1	19
1	4	0	1	19
1	3	2	0	19
1	2	3	1	19
1	1	5	0	19
1	0	6	1	19
0	5	2	0	19
0	3	5	0	19
0	1	8	0	19

3 **a** 6 firsts and 0 seconds
   3 firsts and 4 seconds
   0 firsts and 8 seconds
   b 3 firsts and 4 seconds
   1 first and 9 seconds
   c 3 firsts and 4 seconds
4 2 tries, 1 conversion, 1 penalty, and 1 dropped goal

5 a 6 wins
b 3 ties
c 2 losses
6 [Table 2.14–see page 222]
7 The United States beat the Soviet Union 2–0, the United States beat New Zealand 3–0, Canada beat the United States 1–0, Canada beat the Soviet Union 2–1, New Zealand beat Canada 4–0, and the Soviet Union beat New Zealand 3–1.
8 Kyla definitely hit the bull's eye. If her first shot was only worth 3 points, Kyla would have had to hit the bull's eye in one of her other five shots to make 71 points. Note that if Pedro had hit the bull's eye, his score would have been at least 72 points (not 71).
[Table 2.15–see page 222]

Investigation Three — Using Rates

1 a No. Average speed = total distance ÷ total time, not the mean of the two speeds.
b i

Time (seconds)	
Chicken	**Rabbit**
100	40
100	**200**
200	**240**

ii Average speed = total distance ÷ total time. So for the rabbit the average speed = 800 ÷ 240 m/s = 3.3 m/s (to the nearest tenth).
iii The chicken takes 200 seconds to run the two laps and wins by 40 seconds.
c Suppose the rabbit runs the second lap at 2.5 m/s:

Lap	Time (s)
1	40
2	160
Total	200

Then the chicken and rabbit will each take 200 seconds for the 800 meters. If the rabbit runs the second lap at any speed faster than 2.5 m/s, he will win the race.
d [Table 2.18–see page 222]
2 Cathy takes 5 hours and 36 minutes for the journey, and Dan takes 3 hours for the first 120 miles. That means he must take less than 2 hours and 36 minutes for the remaining 160 miles. His speed for the 160 miles therefore must

be greater than 160 ÷ 2.6 ≈ 61.5 mph. Dan's minumum speed must be just under 62 mph to beat Cathy.
3 a Answers may vary. However, if one uses the speed = distance ÷ time formula, Marilyn's average speed is 6.4 m/s—which is closer to 6 m/s.
b i 200 seconds
ii 50 seconds
c 6.4 m/s
d 6.3 m/s (to the nearest tenth)
e No, since the *actual* length of the track doesn't matter. Suppose the track was k meters long, then the average speed for the six laps in **d** is:

$$\frac{6k}{\frac{k}{5}+\frac{3k}{6}+\frac{2k}{8}} = \frac{6k}{k(\frac{1}{5}+\frac{1}{2}+\frac{1}{4})}$$

$$= \frac{6}{\frac{1}{5}+\frac{1}{2}+\frac{1}{4}}$$

$$\approx 6.3 \text{ m/s}$$

4 a i 50 feet in 1 second; 180,000 feet (or 34.09 miles) in 1 hour
ii 50 feet/s ≈ 34.09 miles per hour
b The car is traveling at 52.3 mph. So the driver:
i will receive a speeding ticket in town.
ii will not receive a speeding ticket on the highway.

On Your Own **Page 40**

Suppose the distance for one lap is d meters. Then the time for the first lap is $\frac{d}{x}$, and the time for the second lap is $\frac{d}{y}$. Over the two laps the average speed is:

$$\frac{2d}{\frac{d}{x}+\frac{d}{y}} = \frac{2}{\frac{1}{x}+\frac{1}{y}} = \frac{2xy}{x+y}$$

$$\frac{2xy}{x+y} = \frac{x+y}{2}$$

Now
$$4xy = (x+y)^2$$
$$4xy = x^2+2xy+y^2$$
$$0 = x^2-2xy+y^2$$
$$0 = (x-y)^2$$
$$0 = x-y$$
$$x = y$$

---

5 a i $\dfrac{14 \text{ hits}}{29 \text{ turns at bat}} \approx 0.483$

ii Yes. It is higher than most professional baseball averages. The only two professional baseball players who batted over .400 were Roger Hornsby in 1925 and Ted Williams in 1941.

b $\dfrac{16 \text{ hits}}{32 \text{ turns at bat}} = 0.500$

6 a i 0.350
ii 0.381
iii 0.353
iv No. Simply averaging the two half-season averages does not reflect the number of times at bat Ted Williams had in each half. His full-season average must take into account the fact that he had many more times at bat in the first half season.

b i 0.340
ii 0.367
iii 0.360
iv The average is 0.354, which does not equal the overall season batting average of 0.360. The only way the *average* of the two half-year batting averages will equal the overall season batting average is if the bottom number in both ratios is equal. You cannot average ratios; you must combine the values and calculate a new decimal equivalent instead.

c i Williams had the higher first- and second-half batting averages.

ii Ruth had the higher season batting average. The two batting average ratios need to be *combined* into a season ratio and then converted into a decimal equivalent. Even though Williams had the better batting averages for both halves of the season, the large number of Williams' times-at-bat during the first half reduced his overall average. Ruth had a better second half of the season when he had many more times-at-bat, which increased his overall season average above Williams'. Therefore, since batting averages are *ratios,* they cannot be averaged like fractions.

CHAPTER TWO — CHECK-UP

1 There are many answers possible. One set of draws could be:**[Table 2.19–see page 222]**
2 **a** Just one way: 1 touchdown and 5 field goals.
b The table shows the points that can be scored.
[Table 2.20–see page 222]
The points that cannot be scored are: 1, 2, 3, 5, 6, 9, 10, 13, 17.
3 2 hours and 39 minutes to the nearest minute.
4 **[Table 2.21–see page 223]**

CHAPTER 3 — DISCOVERING RULES

Investigation One — Rules from Geometric Patterns

1 **a** Answers will vary.
b Suppose you think the rule is $r = 4p$. This means that every post has 4 rails, but since the first post has no rails attached, 4 rails must be deducted.
c i Yes. This rule indicates that you deduct a post and attach 4 rails to the remaining posts.
ii Yes, because $4p - 4 = 4(p - 1)$.
d 68 rails

2 **a**

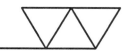

b Each of the basic units requires two matchsticks, and an extra matchstick is needed to close the first triangle. So, $g = 2n + 1$.
c i $m = 3n + 1$
ii $m = 5n + 1$
iii $m = 5n + 1$
iv $m = 4n + 1$
v $m = 6n + 1$
d Yes: $m = x(n - 1) + 1$.

3 **a** $y = 5x + 1$
b Each garden unit looks like this:

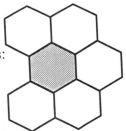

An additional paving stone is required to fill the gap at the beginning of the design.
c 51

4 **a** Pentane:

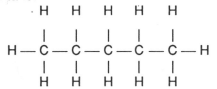

Hexane:

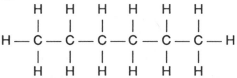

b n units linked together need n carbon atoms and $2n$ hydrogen atoms. An additional hydrogen atom is required at each end of the chain. So $m = 2n + 2$.
c 202

d i Pentene:

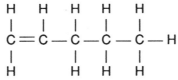

Hexene:

$$H - C = C - C - C - C - C - H$$

(structural formulas for pentene and hexene showing H atoms bonded to each carbon)

ii The formula is C_nH_{2n}, so $m = 2n$.
e The formula is $C_nH_{2(n-1)}$, or C_nH_{2n-2}. So, $m = 2(n-1)$.

On Your Own   **Page 54**

1 Alcohols have the general-class formula $C_nH_{2n+1}OH$. An example is ethyl alcohol, or ethanol, which is represented by:

$$H - C - C - OH$$

(structural formula of ethanol)

2 Aldehydes are made from alcohols and have the general-class formula $C_nH_{2n+1}COH$.

[Table 3.1–see page 223]

3 Fats and oils are energy-storing compounds used by plants and animals. In naturally occurring fats, each molecule is derived from two or three different fatty acids. About 50 fatty acids are found in nature. The vast majority of them have an even number of carbon atoms in their molecules.

[Table 3.2–see page 223]

Fats containing a large proportion of unsaturated acids tend to have low melting points. Many are liquid at room temperature and are called oils. An appropriate general-class formula for fatty acids is $C_{2n}H_{4n}O_2$.

---

5 a i The reasoning is correct. The 18×18 grid contains 17 checkmarks in each of the 18 rows. Altogether there are 18×17 checkmarks, which represent 18×17 games.
ii $18 \times 17 \times \$10{,}000 = \$3{,}060{,}000$
b There are 18×18 checkmarks and ×'s altogether. Each row contains one ×. The 18 rows have 18 ×'s (diagonal), so there are $(18 \times 18) - 18$ checkmarks (games).
c $g = n(n - 1)$; $g = n^2 - n$
6 a $y = 4x - 4$ or $y = 4(x - 1)$

b i In each garden there are x^2 squares. The planting area is $(x - 2)^2$, so $x^2 - (x - 2)^2$ tiles are needed.
ii Yes, because $x^2 - (x - 2)^2 = x^2 - (x^2 - 4x + 4)$
$= x^2 - x^2 + 4x - 4$
$= 4x - 4$.
c Each vertical strip of tiles contains x tiles. So the two vertical strips contain $2x$ tiles. Each horizontal strip of tiles contains $(x - 2)$ tiles. There are $2(x - 2)$ tiles in the two horizontal strips, so the total number of tiles is $2x + 2(x - 2)$.
d $x^2 - (x - 2)^2 = 4x - 4$ (See **6 b ii**.)
$2x + 2(x - 2) = 2x + 2x - 4 = 4x - 4$
7 a No. For a mystic rose with, say, 4 points, there are $(4 \times 3) \div 2$ lines, because each line joins a pair of points.
b $(20 \times 19) \div 2 = 190$ lines.
c $\frac{1}{2}n(n - 1)$ or $n(n - 1) \div 2$

**Investigation Two —
Discovering Linear Rules**

1 a The labor costs are $25 for each hour, so for x hours the labor costs are $\$25x$. Since there is also a $50 basic charge, the total charge is $y = 25x + 50$.
b i $50
ii Some charge is fair to cover the cost of transportation and lost wages. However, a flat charge of $50 may not be fair as it takes no account of the actual traveling time and transportation costs. In addition, there may be other circumstances involved. How was the plumber notified about the job in the first place? Did he inform the potential customer that there would be a $50 basic charge in advance?
c The 25 in $y = 25x + 50$ is a constant or the *difference* in the third column. 50 is the y value when $x = 0$ (zero hours worked).
d i All the differences are 30.
ii $y = 30x + 40$
iii Electrician's Rates: $40 bench charge plus $30 per hour.
2 a $y = 5x + 1$
b $y = 4x + 2$
c $y = 0.5x + 2$
d $y = 0.2x + 2$
e $y = 10x + 10$
f $y = mx + c$
3 a No
b i 15
ii $t = 30w + 15$
iii A turkey that weighs 0 kilograms does not make sense—and it also doesn't make sense to cook nothing for 15 minutes.

c Given the general equation $y = ax + b$, when $x = 1$, $y = a + b$. Since a is the constant difference (30), and $y = 45$ when $x = 1$ in this table, $45 = 30 + b$—which means $b = 15$. Therefore, the correct formula for this situation is $y = 30x + 15$ (or $t = 30w + 15$).

4 a Difference = 4 and $b = 5$. So $s = 4n + 5$

  b i Week 24
  ii Week 21
  iii Week 14
  iv Week 0 represents the week before Mary started her fitness program. Note that this table of differences shows that she did 5 situps during Week 0. In fact, she may have done none at all. This is another situation in which using the table of differences for the general linear equation to find a formula may be a better way to approach a real-world problem.

  c i $6n - 4$
  ii $10n - 9$
  iii $0.1n + 1$
  iv $18 - 2n$
  v $103 - 3n$
  vi $a + (n - 1)\,d$

5 a   i

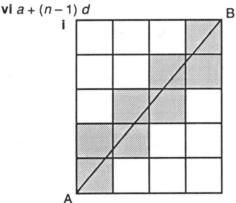

  ii

x	y	Difference
0	$^-2$	
		2
1	0	
		2
2	2	
		2
3	4	
		2
4	6	
		2
5	8	

$$y = 2x - 2$$

  b i $(2 \times 99) - 2 = 196$ broken tiles
  ii $1,960

On Your Own　　　　　　　　**Page 64**

If x and y contain no common factor other than 1, the number of broken tiles is $x + y - 1$. (A 5×3 set of tiles has $5 + 3 - 1$ tiles broken.) As a general rule, if the highest common factor of x and y is h, the number of broken tiles is $x + y - h$. For example, a 6×4 set of tiles has $6 + 4 - 2$ broken tiles and a 9×6 set has $9 + 6 - 3$ broken tiles.

6 a i $t = 4x + 6$
  ii $(4 \times 99) + 6 = 402$
  b i $t = 4(y - 1) + 2$ or $t = 4y + 2$
  ii $t = (4 \times 100) + 2 = 402$
  c Despite using different variables in **a** and **b** above, the answers are the same because $y = x + 1$. So $4y + 2 = 4(x + 1) + 2 = 4x + 4 + 2 = 4x + 6$.

7 a nth term = $5n + 1$
  b

n	n^{th} Term	Difference
0	$^-2$	
		3
1	1	
		3
2	4	
		3
3	7	
		3
4	10	
		3
5	13	

The difference between the second (4) and fifth (13) is 9. Since there are three difference sets between the second and fifth terms, the constant = $9 \div 3 = 3$. The formula for the nth term is $3n - 2$.

8 a i Lucy : $d = 9t$
    Gary : $d = 5t + 50$
    ii Lucy covers 9 meters in every second, so she covers $9t$ meters in t seconds. Gary runs 5 meters every second, so in t seconds he runs $5t$ meters. However, Gary has a 50-meter head start, which means he is $5t + 50$ meters from the start after t seconds.
  b i Line A
  ii Gary reaches the finish line first (after running 10 seconds). It takes Lucy a little more than 11 seconds.
  c A runner's speed is not uniform. It starts at

zero, rises to a maximum, and then falls slightly as the runner tires.

9 a i TeleRent
ii Either company
iii TeleHire

TeleRent is cheaper for short rental periods up to four weeks. However, for periods longer than four weeks, TeleHire is cheaper.

b i TeleHire

w	c	Difference
0	20	
		5
1	25	
		5
2	30	
		5
3	35	
		5
4	40	

ii   TeleRent

w	c	Difference
0	0	
		10
1	10	
		10
2	20	
		10
3	30	
		10
4	40	

c i TeleHire: $c = 5w + 20$
TeleRent : $c = 10w$
ii TeleHire: You pay just $5 a week with a one-time $20 deposit.
TeleRent : No deposit, just $10 per week!

10 a

x	y	Difference
0	300	
		100
1	400	
		100
2	500	
		100
3	600	
		100
4	700	

b i $y = 100x + 300$
ii $x = 8$($80,000 in sales); $y = 800 + 300 =$ $1,100

11 a i

x	y	Difference
0	4	
		3
1	7	
		3
2	10	
		3
3	13	
		3
4	16	

ii $y = 3x + 4$
b $y = 4x + 3$
c i A(4,16); B(4,4); C(0,4)
ii AB = 12, BC = 4
iii 3

d

Coordinates of Points C	AB ÷ BC
(0, 4)	3
(0, 3)	4
(0, 5)	2

e In the general equation, slope = a. In addition, slope is often indicated in the *slope-intercept form:* $y = mx + b$. In this case, slope = m, and (0, b) is the y-intercept.
f Yes, because the triangles ABC in each case are similar to each other—and the slope of the line AC is constant.

12 a $y = \frac{3}{4}x + 2$

b $y = \frac{5}{2}x + 7$

c $y = 2x - 1$

d $y = \frac{1}{2}x + 0.6$

13 a $y = \frac{-2.50}{2}x + 47$

$y = (\frac{-2.50}{2} \times 54) + 47 = -20.5$ minutes

b $y = (-2.50 \times 54) + 47 = -88$ minutes.

Negative time makes no sense in this problem. The formula only works for a narrow band of temperatures (probably within the temperature range shown in the table).

14 a $C = \dfrac{5}{9}(F - 32) \approx \dfrac{5}{9}F - 17.8 \approx 0.556F - 17.8$

b $F = \dfrac{9C}{5} + 32 = 1.8C + 32$

Note: On a graph (F in terms of C), you get these two sets of points:
(0, 32) — C = x-axis
(100, 212) — F = y-axis

Since slope = $\dfrac{y1 - y2}{x1 - x2} = \dfrac{212 - 32}{100 - 0} = \dfrac{180}{100} = \dfrac{9}{5}$

For C in terms of F, the x- and y-axes are reversed.

**Investigation Three —
Discovering Quadratic Rules**

1   a 63 dominoes
b This method provides a solution but is very tedious without using a computer. It's not the best strategy for solving this problem.
c i

x	y	Pattern in y
1	3	1 × 3
2	8	2 × 4
3	15	3 × 5
4	24	4 × 6
5	35	5 × 7
.	.	.
.	.	.
.	.	.
74	5,624	74 × 76
x	y	x × (x + 2)

$y = x(x + 2)$
ii 74 × 76 = 5,624
d $y = x(x + 2) = x^2 + 2x$

2   a i $y = x^2 + 2x$

x	y	First Difference	Second Difference
0	0		
		3	
1	3		2
		5	
2	8		2
		7	
3	15		2
		9	
4	24		2
		11	
5	35		

$y = 2x^2 - 3x + 1$

x	y	First Difference	Second Difference
0	1		
		−1	
1	0		4
		3	
2	3		4
		7	
3	10		4
		11	
4	21		4
		15	
5	36		

ii The second difference is the same—or a constant.

b i

x	y	First Difference	Second Difference
0	−1		
		7	
1	6		2
		9	
2	15		2
		11	
3	26		2
		13	
4	39		

ii

x	y	First Difference	Second Difference
0	9		
		−4	
1	5		8
		4	
2	9		8
		12	
3	21		8
		20	
4	41		

iii

x	y	First Difference	Second Difference
0	4		
		3	
1	7		4
		7	
2	14		4
		11	
3	25		4
		15	
4	40		

iv

x	y	First Difference	Second Difference
0	8		
		5	
1	13		−2
		3	
2	16		−2
		1	
3	17		−2
		−1	
4	16		

c i [Table 3.17–see page 223]
ii The second difference is always $2a$; in other words, it is twice the coefficient of x^2 in the quadratic equation $y = ax^2 + bx + c$.

3 a i The y-values for $x = 0$ are 0 in the first table and c in the second. That means c must be 0.
ii The second difference in the first table is 2. That means $2a$ in the second table is 2, and a must be 1. The initial entry in the first-difference column is 3 in the first table and $a + b$ in the second. Since $a + b = 3$, and $a = 1$, $1 + b = 3$—and $b = 2$.
b Yes, because $y = ax^2 + bx + c$ gives $y = 1x^2 + 2x + 0$, or $x^2 + 2x$.
c $y = x^2 + 4x + 3$

4 a $y = x^2 + 2x + 1$ or $y = (x + 1)^2$
b $y = 2x^2 + 1$
c $y = 3x^2 − x + 1$
d $y = 3x^2 + 2x$
e $y = \frac{1}{2}x^2 + \frac{1}{2}x$
f $y = 6x^2 + 8x + 10$

5 **a** $y = \frac{3}{2}x^2 + \frac{1}{2}x$. Here is the difference table:

x	y	First Difference	Second Difference
0	0		
		2	
1	2		3
		5	
2	7		3
		8	
3	15		3
		11	
4	26		

b 15,050

6 **a** $y = \frac{1}{2}x^2 - \frac{1}{2}x$. Here is the difference table:

x	y	First Difference	Second Difference
0	0		
		0	
1	0		1
		1	
2	1		1
		2	
3	3		1
		3	
4	6		

b 37,401 handshakes among 274 graduates.

7 **a** $y = \frac{1}{2}x^2 + \frac{1}{2}x + 1$. Here is the difference table:

x	y	First Difference	Second Difference
0	1		
		1	
1	2		1
		2	
2	4		1
		3	
3	7		1
		4	
4	11		

b 5,051 regions

8 **a** $y = x^2 + x$
b 1,001,000
c $y = x^2$
d $y = \frac{1}{2}x^2 + \frac{1}{2}x$

e **i** $y = \frac{3}{2}x^2 + \frac{1}{2}x$
 ii $y = 2x^2 - x$
 iii $y = 0.1x^2 + 0.5x$
 iv $y = -\frac{3}{2}x^2 + \frac{203}{2}x$
 v $y = -\frac{1}{2}x^2 + \frac{97}{2}x$
 vi $y = \frac{1}{2}dx^2 + a(-\frac{1}{2}d)x = \frac{1}{2}x(2a + (x-1)d)$

9 **a** $y = \frac{3}{2}x^2 - \frac{1}{2}x$
b 14,950

10 **a** $y = 2x^2 - x$
b 19,900

11 a If $x = 5$, then $y = 5^3 - 3^3 = 98$.
 b **i** When $x = 6$, $y = 6^3 - 4^3 = 152$.
 ii When $x = 7$, $y = 7^3 - 5^3 = 218$.
 iii When $x = 8$, $y = 8^3 - 6^3 = 296$.
 iv When $x = 12$, $y = 12^3 - 10^3 = 728$.
 c For a $5 \times 5 \times 5$ cube there are a total of 5^3 cubes. If 3^3 of these are unpainted, $5^3 - 3^3$ cubes are painted. That is, $5^3 - (5-2)^3$ cubes are painted. So, for a large cube of side x, there are a total of x^3 cubes and $(x-2)^3$ unpainted cubes. If y is the number of painted cubes, $y = x^3 - (x-2)^3$.

d

x	y	First Difference	Second Difference
0	8		
		−6	
1	2		12
		6	
2	8		12
		18	
3	26		12
		30	
4	56		12
		42	
5	98		12
		54	
6	152		

$y = 6x^2 - 12x + 8$

e Yes, because $x^3 - (x-2)^3 = x^3 - x^3 - (x^3 - 6x^2 + 12x - 8) = x^3 - x^3 + 6x^2 - 12x + 8 = 6x^2 - 12x + 8$.

f i $z = 8$, for $x \geq 2$. Here is the table:

x	z
2	8
3	8
4	8
5	8
6	8

ii $u = 12x - 24$ for $x \geq 2$. Here is the difference table:

x	u	Difference
0	-24	
		12
1	-12	
		12
2	0	
		12
3	12	
		12
4	24	
		12
5	36	
		12
6	48	

iii $w = 6x^2 - 24x + 24$ for $x \geq 2$. Here is the difference table:

x	w	First Difference	Second Difference
0	-24		
		-18	12
1	-6		
		-6	12
2	0		
		6	12
3	6		
		18	12
4	24		
		30	12
5	54		
		42	12
6	96		

g $w + u + z = (6x^2 - 24x + 24) + (12x - 24) + 8 = 6x^2 - 12x + 8$

On Your Own   Page 83

1

Number of Frogs of Each Color	Minimum Number of Moves
1	3
2	8
3	15
4	24

2 For n frogs of each color, there are $n(n + 2) = n^2 + 2n$ moves.

3 [Table 3.26–see page 223]

So for n frogs of each color, the minimum number of moves requires $2n$ hops to adjacent unused pads and n^2 jumps over a frog to an unused pad.

**Investigation Four —
Exploring More Complex Rules**

1   **a i** 100 oranges in the 10th layer
      ii 385 oranges in the pyramid
   b i [Table 3.27—see page 224]
      ii A linear equation has a constant first difference and a quadratic has a constant second difference. In this table, the third differences are constant, which suggests that this is a cubic equation of the form $y = ax^3 + bx^2 + cx + d$.

iii [Table 3.28–see page 224]

iv If you match the numbers from Joe's table with the general table, $6a = 2$, so $a = \frac{1}{3}$. Also, $6a + 2b = 3$, so $b = \frac{1}{2}$. For the first difference, $a + b + c = 1$, so $c = \frac{1}{6}$. When $x = 0$, $y = d = 0$. Therefore, to predict the number of oranges (y) in a square pyramid, use this equation: $y = \frac{1}{3}x^3 + \frac{1}{2}x^2 + \frac{1}{6}x$.

v Yes, because $\frac{1}{3}x^3 + \frac{1}{2}x^2 + \frac{1}{6}x = \frac{1}{6}x(2x^2 + 3x + 1)$. Joe might also note that he used the $1^2 + 2^2 + \cdots + n^2$ formula to come up with the numbers in his difference table.

2 **a** The number of squares on an 8×8 chess-board is $1^2 + 2^2 + 3^2 + \ldots + 8^2 = 204$.

b Based on 1, $1^2 + 2^2 + 3^2 + \ldots + n^2 = \frac{1}{6}n(n + 1)(2n + 1)$ or $y = \frac{1}{3}x^3 + \frac{1}{2}x^2 + \frac{1}{6}x$.

On Your Own   **Page 87**

[Table 3.29–see page 224]
[Table 3.30–see page 224]

$1 + 2 + 3 + 4 + \ldots + n = \frac{1}{2}n(n + 1)$

So $(1 + 2 + 3 + 4 + \ldots + n)^2 = (\frac{1}{2}n(n + 1))^2 = \frac{1}{4}n^2(n + 1)^2$.

---

3 $y = \frac{1}{3}x^3 + x^2 + \frac{2}{3}x = \frac{1}{3}x(x + 1)(x + 2)$

4 $y = \frac{1}{6}x^3 + \frac{1}{2}x^2 + \frac{1}{3}x = \frac{1}{6}x(x + 1)(x + 2)$

5 **a** $y = x^3 + x = x(x^2 + 1)$
  b $y = 2x^3 - x = x(2x^2 - 1)$
  c $y = x^3 + x^2 + x = x(x^2 + x + 1)$
  d $y = 3x^2 - x^3 = x^2(3 - x)$
  e $y = 5x^2 - x^3 = x^2(5 - x)$
  f $y = x^3 - x^2 + 8$

6 **a** $y = \frac{1}{4}n^4 + \frac{1}{2}n^3 + \frac{1}{4}n^2 = \frac{1}{4}n^2(n + 1)^2 = [\frac{1}{2}n(n + 1)]^2$

  b **i** $y = \frac{1}{3}n^3 + n^2 + \frac{2}{3}n = \frac{1}{3}n(n + 1)(n + 2)$

    ii $y = \frac{1}{3}n^3 - \frac{1}{3}n = \frac{1}{3}n(n - 1)(n + 1)$

iii $y = \frac{1}{4}n^4 + \frac{5}{6}n^3 + \frac{3}{4}n^2 + \frac{1}{6}n$
$= \frac{1}{12}n(n + 1)(n + 2)(3n + 1)$

7 **a** 31 regions for 6 points.

  b $y = \frac{1}{24}x^4 - \frac{1}{4}x^3 + \frac{23}{24}x^2 - \frac{3}{4}x + 1$
$= \frac{1}{24}(x^4 - 6x^3 + 23x^2 - 18x + 24)$

CHAPTER THREE — CHECK-UP

1 **a** Each unit is shown in this sketch:

An additional match is used to close each design. So the formula is
$y = 6x + 1$

  b $x = 80$, $y = 481$

2 **a**

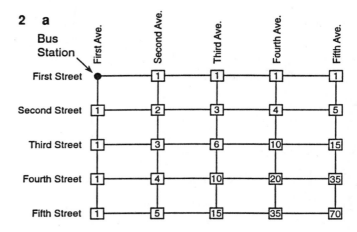

  b **i** $y = 1$ way
    ii $y = n$ ways
    iii $y = \frac{1}{2}n(n + 1)$ ways or $\frac{1}{2}n^2 + \frac{1}{2})n$ ways
    iv $y = \frac{1}{6}n(n + 1)(n + 2)$ ways or

$\frac{1}{6}n^3 + \frac{1}{2}n^2 + \frac{1}{3}n$ ways

    v $y = \frac{1}{6}n(n + 1)(n + 2)$ ways or

$\frac{1}{6}n^3 + \frac{1}{2}n^2 + \frac{1}{3}n$ ways

Chapter 4
EXPLORING RATES

Investigation One — Uniform Rates

1 **a i** 12 mm
   ii 12 mm
   iii 12 mm
  b Yes. The rate is 12 millimeters/second.
  c

t (s)	d (mm)	Pattern
0	0	12×0
1	12	12×1
2	24	12×2
3	36	12×3
4	**4 8**	12×4
t	d	$12 \times t$

$$d = 12 \times t$$

  d The 12 in $d = 12 \times t$ represents 12 mm/s,
which is the rate or speed of carpet production.
  e i 13 mm/s
   ii 8.7 mm/s
   iii 18.4 mm/s
2 **a** $2.50 per lb.
  b $p = 2.50w$. Note that the 2.50 in the formula is
the cost per pound.
3 **a** 0.5 gallons/hour
  b Because the concrete mixer turns at a constant rate, it uses fuel at a constant rate.
  c i [Table 4.2–see page 225]
  ii The 0.5 in the equation $p = 0.5t$ represents
the rate of fuel consumption.
  iii

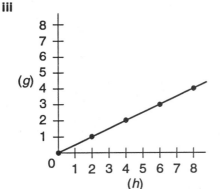

Yes, the equation is linear (of the form $y = ax
+ b$). 0.5, or the rate of fuel consumption, is
represented by the slope of the line. Note that
b is 0, because when $x = 0$, $y = 0$.
  d [Table 4.3–see page 225]

4 **a** 240,000 joules/120 seconds = 2,000 joules/
second
  b 1 joule/second = 1 watt. So 2,000 joules/
second = 2,000 watts = 2 kilowatts.
  c $E = 2t$
  d i 3.1 kw
   ii 0.9 kw
   iii 2.6 kw
5 **a** $d = 15t$
  b

Runner	Speed (s) km/h	Formula
1	15	$d = 15t$
2	17	$d = 17t$
3	8	$d = 8t$
4	11	$d = 11t$
5	**7.3**	$d = 7.3t$
6	**14.8**	$d = 14.8t$
7	**11.5**	$d = 11.5t$
8	5	$d = 5t$

On Your Own   **Page 97**

  If the power rating is not given in kilowatts, it can
be worked out by using the formula: Power
(watts) = Voltage (volts) × Current (amps).
Remember that 1,000 watts = 1 kilowatt. Heaters
usually contribute most to the average home
electricity bill.

---

6 **a** $C = 21.49 + 3.00$
  b i [Table 4.5–see page 225]
  ii Your school should buy from Brown & Brown
because that firm offers a relatively cheap
price for such low postage.
  iii Your school should buy from Cheapsales
because that firm offers the cheapest price per
calculator. The relatively high price of postage
is not much when the number of calculators to
be bought and shipped is so large.
  c $C = 6n + 84$
7 **a** $d_{front} = 20t$
  b $d_{end} = 20t - 60$
  c 35 meters
  d 43 seconds
  e i 80 meters
   ii 16 m/s
  f 55 seconds

8 a [Table 4.6–see page 226]
b For a 100-meter race, everyone will cross the finish line in about 11 seconds.

9 a 18 seconds
b 162 meters
c 18 meters from the starting line
d Joanne: 10 meters from the start
Mary: 20 meters from the start
Jules: 30 meters from the start
e 25 meters from the start
f There is no guarantee of a tie, but the runners should be quite close to each other.

10 a $d = 15t$

b i 1 foot takes $\frac{1}{15}$, or 0.0666666 seconds.

ii 1 mile takes 351.9996 seconds, which is approximately 5 minutes and 52 seconds at Rosa's speed. (1 mile = 5,280 feet, so it takes 5,280 times the answer in problem **b i**.)

c about 2 hours and 34 minutes

d i [Table 4.7–see page 226]

ii The products = 1 because they are reciprocals. (Note that the answers shown on a calculator may be very close to 1 because of round-off error when dividing or multiplying.)

e i

Speed (ft/s)	Rate (/ft)
4.3	0.23
11.6	0.086
0.962	1.04
5.814	0.17

ii

Speed (ft/s)	Rate (s/ft)
20.37	0.0491
15.87	0.063
0.747	1.339
1.390	0.7194

11 a

t	d	Difference
0	0	
		3
1	3	
		9
2	12	
		15
3	27	
		21
4	48	
		27
5	75	
		30
6	105	
		30
7	135	
		30
8	165	

First differences are not constant until $t = 5$ (that is, until the car has gotten 5 seconds away from the stoplight). So the speed was not constant throughout the car's journey from the stoplight.
b i 30 feet per second ≈ 20.45 miles per hour
ii $d = 30t - 75$, $t \geq 5$.
iii $d = 3t^2$, $t \leq 5$.
iv When $t \leq 5$ seconds, the graph shows a curve, not a line. In fact, the equation for $t \leq 5$ represents a quadratic function, not a linear one. However, for $t \geq 5$ the slope is constant to match the linear equation $d = 30t - 75$.

On Your Own   **Page 102**

1 This runner should plan for a rate of 5.11 minutes/mile. Minutes per mile is used, since a marathoner gauges his or her running pace based on predetermined times for *splits* (segments of a race course, usually three-mile splits for marathons) that are clocked on a stopwatch. It is easier for a runner to keep track of the number of minutes it takes to run one mile than to calculate the speed he or she is running in miles/minute or miles/hour.
2 On a perfectly flat course with no wind, marathoners should plan to run at a constant rate, since this is the most economical way to use a given amount of energy. In practice, courses are seldom flat and wind is often a factor. So a marathoner has to plan different rates for different parts of the course.

3 In cycling, riders shelter, or "draft," behind other riders to conserve energy. Cyclists who try to break from the bunch to get a winning advantage have to work harder and hence are invariably caught by the bunch. So the overall speed is determined by tactics rather than trying to maintain a constant speed.

4 Swimmers move close to constant speeds in races, since these races take place in pools where variables such as water temperature, currents, and obstacles are controlled.

Investigation Two — Changing Rates

1 **a i** 16 feet/second
  ii 48 feet/second
  iii 80 feet/second
  iv 112 feet/second
  b The average speed in **a** increases by 32 feet/second for consecutive intervals of one second. So the average speed during the fifth second would be 112 + 32 = 144 feet/second.
  c i The average speed is greater than (>) the speed at exactly 5 seconds.
    ii The average speed is less than (<) the speed at exactly 6 seconds.
  d i

Time Interval (t)	Average Speed (d)	Difference
0th	⁻16	
		32
1st	16	
		32
2nd	48	
		32
3rd	80	
		32
4th	112	
		32
5th	144	
		32
6th	176	

The average speed = $32t - 16$. During the twentieth second, the average speed = 624 feet/second, which equals approximately 425 miles/hour. Note that the first time interval is from 0 to 1 second. To construct an imaginary 0th time interval for the finite-differences procedure, think about the average speed from ⁻1 to 0 seconds. Imagine that the parachutist starts at 0 seconds and "falls up": At ⁻1 second,

average speed would be the negative of the average speed during the first time interval (16 feet/second). Therefore, $d = -16$ for the 0 time interval of 0 to ⁻1 seconds.
  ii The impact of raindrops falling at 425 miles/hour would be similar to that of bullets and would kill most animals and plants. Therefore, raindrops do not reach such speeds as they fall. In fact, their speed is slowed by air resistance—as would be the speed of a falling parachutist.
  e i The graph indicates that after about 5 seconds, raindrops fall close to a constant speed, which is referred to as *terminal velocity*.
    ii Terminal velocity is a constant speed and occurs when air resistance (an upward force) balances the downward force of gravity. For this to happen, air resistance must change with speed; resistance reaches a maximum (the force of gravity) at the terminal velocity. Terminal velocity varies for objects of different size and shape. For a human, it is about 135 miles/hour; terminal velocity is much less for raindrops, since they are smaller, lighter, and slowed down more as they push through the air.

2 **a** $x = 3t^2$
  b During the third hour (from $t = 2$ to $t = 3$) the area covered by floodwaters changes from 12 to 27 acres. So the average rate of flooding during the third hour is 15 acres/hour.
  c Between $t = 2$ and $t = 4$, $48 - 12 = 36$ acres are covered with floodwater. During this two-hour period, the average rate of flooding is $36 \div 2$, or 18 acres/hour.
  d 33 acres/hour
  e The flooding equation in **a** is unrealistic, since the flood will reach its peak and then recede as the rain stops. Also, the height of the flood will be affected by the tide; incoming tides are known as the "flood tides," and outgoing ones are called "ebb tides."

3 **a** $A = 2t^2$
  b i 200 mm^2
    ii 242 mm^2
    iii 42 mm^2/second
  c The average rate of increase for the area of the blot will slow down as the ink is absorbed, so it's not appropriate to use $A = 2t^2$ for all values of t.

4 **a** $P = 100n^3$
  b i $1,900 per year
    ii $9,100 per year

5 **a** $d = 4t^2$
  b $y = \frac{1}{2}x^2$
  c $V = 2x^3$
  d $T = 4x^3$

6 a The distance traveled between $t = 0.5$ and $t = 1$ is 6.25 meters. The average speed during this time interval (half a second) is $6.25 \div 0.5 = 12.5$ meters/second.

b [Table 4.12–see page 226]

c A negative average speed indicates that the ball is coming down.

d The formula is $d = 20t - 5t^2$. Note: This formula is based on the following table:

t	d	First Difference	Second Difference
0	0		
		15	
1	15		−10
		5	
2	20		−10
		−5	
3	15		−10
		−15	
4	0		

e The ball is slowing down because the difference between the distances measured decreases for successive time intervals. In other words, the ball travels smaller and smaller distances as time goes on—which means its average speed is decreasing.

7 a Since the distance the ball rolls in successive time intervals is increasing, the ball speeds up as it goes down the slope.

b

Time(t) (seconds)	Ball (d) (meters	Car's Distance (meter)
0	0	0
1	2	8
2	8	16
3	18	**24**
4	**32**	**32**
5	**50**	**40**

c i The car is ahead.
  ii The car is ahead.
  iii The car is ahead.
  iv The car and ball have traveled an equal distance.
  v The ball is ahead.

d If you average the distance the ball travels in the intervals 0–1, 1–2, 2–3, and 3–4 seconds—($2 + 6 + 10 + 14) \div 4$—the result is 8 meters/second. This is the constant speed of the car. In other words, the total distance (32 meters) traveled by each in the first four seconds is the same.

8 a Yes. For successive one-second intervals, the average speed is 1 meter/second, 3 meters/second, 5 meters/second, 7 meters/second, and 9 meters/second. That means the wrench is speeding up as it falls.

b i 21 meters
  ii 3 seconds
  iii 7 meters/second

c [Table 4.15–see page 227]

d Average speed $= \dfrac{d_2 - d_1}{t_2 - t_1}$

9 a Yes. The actual amount of water flowing through the break in the levee in successive one-second intervals is 5 m^3, 15 m^3, 25 m^3, 35 m^3, and 45 m^3. That means the average rate of water flowing through the break is increasing.

b i 105 m^3
  ii 35 m^3/second

c [Table 4.16–see page 227]

d i $w = 5t^2$
  ii 100 seconds

**Investigation Three —
Instantaneous Rates**

1 a Yes. The distances moved in successive seconds are 6, 18, 30, 42, and 54 feet, so the car is accelerating.

b During the seventh second, the car travels 78 feet. The average speed during this interval is 78 feet/second, or about 53 miles/hour. During the eighth second the average speed is 90 feet/second, or about 61 miles/hour. Since the posted speed limit is 50 mph, the driver should expect to get a speeding ticket if the pattern continues.

c $d = 6t^2$

d i The distance traveled during the time interval $t = 2.9$ to $t = 3$ seconds is $(6 \times 3^2) - (6 \times 2.9^2)$ feet.

So the average speed is $\dfrac{(6 \times 3^2) - (6 \times 2.9^2)}{3 - 2.9}$.

ii 35.4 feet/second, or about 24 miles/hour. The average speed for this instant is higher because the Porsche is accelerating. The speed of an accelerating car is much higher at the end of an interval than the beginning—that is, as it approaches a limit. Therefore, the average speed of 30 feet/second for the entire one-second interval does not accurately reflect the problem.

iii [Table 4.17–see page 228]

iv Because calculators can only compute values to the maximum design accuracy of the machine when doing arithmetic, calculator answers become unreliable as the time interval gets very small. However, by extending the pattern found in problem **d iii**, the table can be completed:

Time Before Seeing Officer (seconds)	Average Speed (feet/seconds)
2.9	35.4
2.99	35.94
2.999	35.994
2.9999	35.9994
2.99999	**35.99994**
2.999999	**35.999994**
2.9999999	**35.9999994**
2.99999999	**35.99999994**
2.999999999	**35.999999994**

v The pattern in the table suggests that the instantaneous speed at exactly 3 seconds is 36 feet/second.
vi No. 36 feet/second $\approx$ 24.5 miles/hour, which does not come close to 50 miles/hour.
e i 96 feet/second
ii Yes. The driver would be traveling at about 65 miles/hour.
2 a 25 meters/second
b $d = 5t^2$
c [Table 4.19–see page 228]
d 30 meters/second
e Yes. The speed at 3 seconds is 30 meters/second, which is more than the 28 meters/second speed necessary to break the concrete.
f Yes, it matters. If the operator bases the calculation of average speed on the 25 meters/second traveled between 2 and 3 seconds, then it looks like the ball won't go fast enough at 3 seconds to smash the concrete. However, the instantaneous speed of 30 meters/second based on the formula and the second table should work.
3 a $d = 1.5t^2$
b The speed at 5 seconds is 15 feet/second.
c The bumper won't need to be repaired because the speed at collision is less than the 24 feet/second necessary for significant damage.
4 a $n = 1,000t^2$
b The rate is 12,000 fruit flies per week.

c 10,000,000 fruit flies. This doesn't make sense, because it assumes absolutely no deaths. In fact, most fruit flies will be eaten by predators or die from poor weather conditions.
5 a i $d = t^2$, $s = 2t$
ii $d = 3t^2$, $s = 6t$
iii $d = 0.5t^2$, $s = 1t$
b In the distance formula, the coefficient of t^2 is half of the coefficient of t in the speed formula. In other words, speed is the constant difference in such second-degree difference tables—or 2a.
c i

d	s
t^2	$2t$
$3t^2$	$6t$
$0.5t^2$	t
$5t^2$	$10t$
at^2	**$2at$**

ii

d	s
$11t^2$	**$22t$**
$7t^2$	**$14t$**
$4t^2$	**$8t$**
$20t^2$	**$40t$**
$100t^2$	**$200t$**

iii

d	s
$6t + 4$	6
$11t - 8$	**11**
$14t$	**14**
7	**0**
$bt + c$	**b**

Note that s in the case of these linear equations is equal to the slope of the line.

6 b i $\dfrac{[\frac{1}{2}(3.9)^2 + 3(3.9) + 1] - [\frac{1}{2}(4)^2 + 3(4) + 1]}{0.1 \text{ seconds}} =$
6.95 meters/second

ii Based on the next table, the instantaneous speed is 7 meters/second.

[Table 4.23–see page 228]

c i

t	s
0	3
1	4
2	5
3	6
4	7

ii $s = t + 3$

d i $s = t$

ii $s = 3$

iii $s = 0$

e If the sum of $d = \frac{1}{2}t^2$, $d = 3t$, and $d = 1$ is $d = \frac{1}{2}t^2 + 3t + 1$, then you can also combine the related speed formulas: $s = t + 3 + 0 = t + 3$.

7 a $s = 10t + 3 + 0 = 10t + 3$

b $s = 6t + 4 + 0 = 6t + 4$

c $s = 8t - 2 - 0 = 8t - 2$

8 a $p = 5.6 + 2t - 0.1t^2$

$s = 0 + 2 - 0.2t = 2 - 0.2t$

b

t (weeks)	Rate ($/week)
0	2
2	1.6
4	1.2
6	0.8
8	0.4
10	0
12	−0.4
14	−0.8

c A negative rate indicates that the share price is falling.

d i When the rate of change is zero. That's because the share price is highest then—but is about to start falling.

ii $t = 10$ weeks

e When the price graph is at its highest point, the rate-of-change graph goes to $r = 0$; it crosses the t-axis at $t = 10$.

ON YOUR OWN   PAGE 119

This equation may have been constructed by using the finite-differences procedure on share values for the past several months. Mathematicians have also developed computer techniques (for example, regression analysis) to uncover such equations.

9 a The graph for $t \le 4$ shows $s = \frac{9 \text{ meters}}{4 \text{ seconds}} t$ or $s = 2.25t$. The related formula for distance is therefore $d = \frac{1}{2}(2.25)t^2 = 1.125t^2$.

b i 18 meters

ii For $t \ge 4$, $s = 9$. Since the runner goes at the same speed at 4 seconds and beyond, the formula can be written as a linear equation. So $d = 9t + c$, where c is a constant. As shown in **b i**, when $t = 4$, $d = 18$. Therefore, $18 = 9 \times 4 + c$ and $c = -18$. The distance equation is $d = 9t - 18$, in which the constant represents the 18 meters the runner ran from 0–4 seconds.

Investigation Four — Maxima and Minima

1 a

t	h
0	0
0.2	0.8
0.4	**1.2**
0.6	**1.2**
0.8	**0.8**
1.0	**0**

b i The weight is at its maximum height at 0.5 seconds. That's because the height at 0.4 and 0.6 seconds is the same (1.2). The height at 0.5 seconds must be higher in order to fall back to 1.2 meters at 0.6 seconds. Here is the graph:

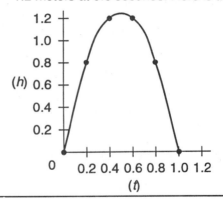

ii 1.25 meters

c i $s = 5 - 10t$

ii $s = 0$

iii $s = 5 - 10t = 0$. So $t = 0.5$ seconds. Here is the graph:

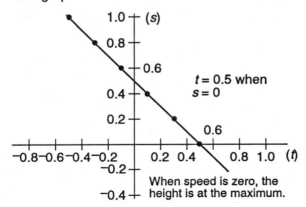

$t = 0.5$ when $s = 0$

When speed is zero, the height is at the maximum.

d 5 meters. The speed equation for $h = 10t - 5t^2$ is $s = 10 - 10t$. If $s = 0$ at the maximum height, then $0 = 10 - 10t = 1$ second. Use this value of t in the distance formula, and $h = 10 - 5 = 5$ meters.

e The speed formula should be considerably easier than using table patterns.

2 a Here's one example: If $t = 2$, then $h = 60 - 20 = 40$, which matches the table of values.

b $s = 30 - 10t$

c If $s = 0$ at the arrow's maximum height, then $0 = 30 - 10t$, and $t = 3$ seconds.

d 45 meters

3 a 4.5

b 90

c 12.5

d 101

4 a Here's one example: If $t = 0.2$, then $h = 0.2 - 0.8 + 1 = 0.4$, which matches the table of values.

b $s = 10t - 4$

c Since the yo-yo drops and rises again in an interval of 0.8 seconds, it reaches the minimum height above the ground at half of that inverval— or at $t = 0.4$ seconds. (This assumes the yo-yo moves at a constant speed.) If $s = 0$ when the minimum height is reached, then the yo-yo stops moving at 0.4 seconds.

d 0.2 meters

5 a 8

b 3

c 5

d 2.75

6 a The maximum distance $d = 100$ at $t = 10$.

b [Table 4.27–see p.228]

c i The area of a rectangle is $A = xy$. Since $y = 20 - x$, $A = x(20 - x)$.

ii $A = x(20 - x) = 20x - x^2$

d Find a rate formula to determine the maximum area (a): rate $= 20 - 20x$. When rate $= 0$, $x = 10$ meters. Since $y = 20 - x$, $y = 10$ meters. So, the maximum area $= 100$ meters^2 when $x = y = 10$ meters. The floor with the largest possible area is a square.

7 a The distance formula is quadratic because the difference between intervals varies. However, the speed formula is linear because the *rate of change* it represents is constant (as shown by the slope of the line).

b i [Table 4.28–see p.229]

ii $A = xy = x(200 - 2x) = 200x - 2x^2$

iii Find the linear equation that goes with the Area formula: rate $= 200 - 4x$. When rate $= 0$, $x^2 = 50$ yards. Since $y = 200 - 2x$, $y = 100$ yards in the maximum case. So $A = 50$ yards $\times 100$ yards $= 5,000$ yards^2.

iv The box on the x-axis is 50, and the Area-axis (A) box is 5,000—in other words, the highest point on the curve (which is a graph of the Area formula) represents the maximum area.

8 a

y (vertical)	Pattern in y
400	400 − (2 × 0)
380	400 − (2 × 10)
360	400 − (2 × 20)
340	400 − (2 × 30)
320	400 − (2 × 40)
y	400 − (2 × x)

b $A = xy = x(400 - 2x) = 400x - 2x^2$

c The maximum area $= 20,000$ cm^2 when $x = 100$ and $y = 200$.

9 a

n (tickets)	Pattern in n
380	680 − (2 × 150)
360	680 − (2 × 160)
340	680 − (2 × 170)
320	680 − (2 × 180)
300	680 − (2 × 190)
n	680 − (2 × c)

b "Total revenue" refers to the price of a ticket (c) multiplied by the number of tickets (n). So $T = cn = c(680 - 2c) = 680c - 2c^2$.

c Maximum revenue comes in when $680 - 4c = 0$, which is when $c = 170$ dollars/ticket.

ON YOUR OWN   **PAGE 125**

Here are examples of natural phenomena that can be represented by quadratic equations: 1) the length of a pendulum and the rate of its swing; 2) the speed of a falling object; and 3) the area of a circle as its diameter increases.

CHAPTER FOUR — CHECK-UP

1 **a** Greenwood: $c = 7n + 9$
    Norfolk: $c = 8.50n$
  b Norfolk is P and Greenwood is Q.
  c i Rex buys from Greenwood when he needs 6 or more bags.
    ii He buys from Norfolk when the number of bags is 6 or fewer.

2 **a** $d = 3t^2$
  b 21 meters/second
  c The average speeds in time intervals of 0.1 second, 0.01 second, and 0.001 second before 4 seconds are 23.7, 23.97, and 23.997 meters/second. This suggests that the instantaneous speed at $t = 4$ is 24 meters/second.

3 **a** Here's one example: If $t = 4$, then $d = 16 + 64 - 32 = 48$, which matches the table of values.
  b The average speeds in time intervals of 0.1 second, 0.01 second, and 0.001 second before 6 seconds are 27.9 feet/second, 27.99 feet/second, and 27.999 feet/second. This suggests that the instantaneous speed at $t = 6$ is 28 feet/second.
  c $s = 2t + 16$

4 **a i** Altogether there are 16 paving stones with an edge along the garden edge. (Note that one paving stone is in the corner.) Since there is a total of 16 stones, the width $y = 16 - x$, where x is the number of stones in the length. So
      Area = length × width
        = $x \times (16 - x)$
        = $x(16 - x)$
    ii $x(16 - x) = 16x - x^2$
  b Find the rate equation that goes with the Area formula: rate = $16 - 2x$. When rate = 0, $x = 8$ feet. Since $y = 16 - x$, $y = 8$ feet also. So the garden with maximum area will be 8 ft × 8 ft—a square with 8 paving stones along each edge and one in the corner.

Chapter 5   USING MAPS

Investigation One — Orienteering

1 **a** She thinks the map is upside down because the approach to the summit of the hill on the left of Kathleen's view is gradual, which means the

contour lines representing this hill on the map should be spaced farther apart. The contours surrounding summit C on the right correspond to this. Similarly, the contours surrounding E represent the steep summit at the right of her view.

b i

ii

iii

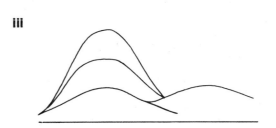

2 **a**

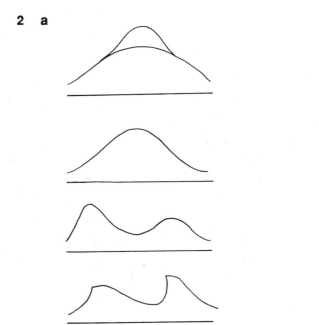

b i Walk to the right along the 80-foot contour. Then go diagonally to Q as you walk to the right of the higher hill.
    ii Immediately climb to the 120-foot contour and walk directly toward R along this contour. You will head down when you've passed the hill.

3 a

b i

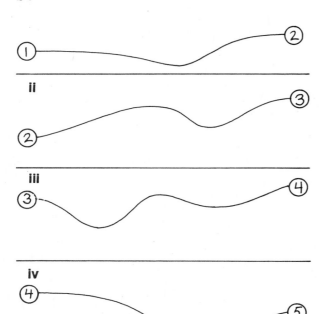

ii

iii

iv

c There are several sensible routes. One is shown by the dotted line.
[Fig 2–see page 229]

4 a All compasses point to magnetic north. Orienteering maps are marked to show magnetic north, not true north, so that magnetic compasses can be used more easily.
b A grid system is a network of parallel lines that intersect at right angles and produce a series of identical squares on a map. Grid lines are numbered so that each square and any point in that square can be located with reference to an origin. Although the south-north lines are all parallel, only the south-north line that passes through the origin coincides with *true north*. This particular grid line is known as *grid north*. The remaining south-north grid lines diverge from

true north by various small amounts. That's because maps (even of a small area) represent the curved surface of the earth on a flat piece of paper.

Investigation Two — Shortest Routes

1 a When successive 20° latitudes that are equidistant on the globe are projected onto a cylinder, the distances between adjacent latitudes are no longer equidistant. The following diagram illustrates the extent of the distortion away from the equator.

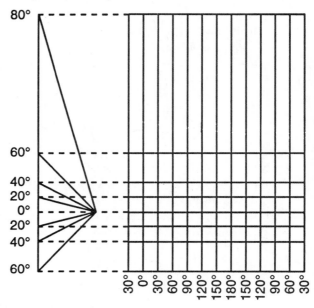

Above 80°N, the distortion is too great to be of any practical use. Antarctica is the only large land mass south of 60°S, and a different kind of map is used to represent it sensibly.
b The Mercator projection progressively enlarges the areas as you move away from the equator. Greenland is much farther from the equator than Australia, and therefore its area is greatly exaggerated.

2 b iv Shortest routes can be found by drawing straight lines on this flattened cylinder world as long as the cut through the cylinder is *not* made between the start and finish. Otherwise, the distance between the two points (B and C) is far too long.
c Mercator maps often have different "cylinder cuts" to ensure that the area of major interest to map users is not divided, which sometimes makes finding shortest routes difficult.

3 b

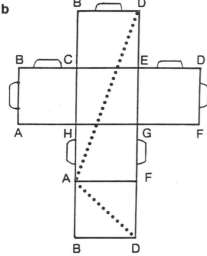

c

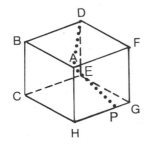

d The straight line represented by A to E on the flat-box diagram represents the longest straight-line route that the ant can walk. If the side of the cube is 1 unit, according to the Pythagorean theorem $AE = \sqrt{1^2 + 2^2} = \sqrt{5}$ units ≈ 2.24 units.

4 a i–ii

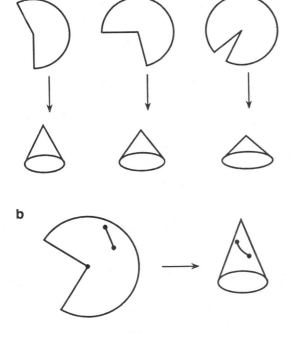

b

You can find shortest routes by collapsing the cone into a flat circle, which is divided into sectors. (Each sector is the same size—the size it takes to make a cone of a particular height.) The shortest route on the surface of a cone is represented by the straight line drawn from start to finish across the appropriate sector. To determine shortest routes on Mt. Fuji, the engineer would use a "collapsed" map of the mountain.

5 a Unfold the fan, lay it flat, and join the two points with a straight line.
b Lay the paper flat, join the two points with a straight line, and measure the length of the line.

On Your Own **Page 141**

1 c The engineer uses a belt like this because it wears evenly on both sides.
2 Cut the strip at one of the points and measure from the cut to the other point.
3 a The result is a single strip.
b One long loop with two twists (not a Möbius strip), intertwined with a short loop that is another Möbius strip.

---

6 a An azimuthal map is constructed by projecting each point on the globe onto a plane that touches the surface at one point. Think of the globe punched with thousands of holes and a light at the center projecting these points onto a plane that touches the surface at one point. Arcs (azimuths) of all the "Great Circles" passing through the point of contact (the center of the map) are projected as straight lines on the map.
b ii *X:* 40°, *Y:* 100°, *Z:* 160°
iii She will have to change bearing (direction) constantly.
c i All bearings are 90°, which means they are the same—in contrast to the different bearings in **b ii**.
ii Yes, because it is easy to follow a constant bearing.

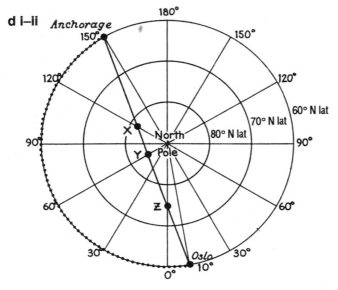

d i–ii *Anchorage*

iii The route via U, V, and W looks significantly longer on the azimuthal map.

e If the origin of a route is the "pole" (center) of an azimuthal map, this map will definitely provide the shortest route. In fact, an azimuthal map will give very nearly the shortest route provided the route goes near the map's pole. Unfortunately, this requires constant changes in bearings by an airplane pilot. A Mercator map severely distorts true distance near the pole, so should never be used in this case. If the route goes over the pole, the Mercator projection is totally useless, since this projection can *never* show the north or south poles. However, there are other instances (such as the Anchorage-to-Oslo example) in which Mercator maps provide practical—if not the shortest—routes to follow.

7 a ii Yes. The Great Circle route appears as a straight line on the azimuthal map.

b ii The Great Circle route is much shorter, so it will be more fuel efficient.

c No. The straight-line route from Perth to Buenos Aires does not pass through Auckland, which is the "pole" for this azimuthal map. The navigator would need a new azimuthal map with Perth at the center for the straight-line route to represent the fuel-efficient Great Circle route.

Investigation Three — Longitude

1 a The Greenwich Observatory was established in the year 1675 for the purpose of calculating longitude. From that time on the Greenwich meridian, which passes through the Observatory, has been recognized by most nations as the prime meridian—or 0° longitude.

b 08:40 hours is the time in Accra, Ghana, also, since Accra and Greenwich are both on the prime meridian (or close enough).

c i–iii *Meridian:* A "Great Circle" that passes through the poles and any place on the earth. *A.M.:* Stands for *ante meridiem* in Latin. A period of time prior to local noon (when the sun is at its highest point), during which the sun is climbing to its highest position. *P.M.:* Stands for *post meridiem* in Latin. A period of time after local noon, during which the sun is descending. Note: Strictly speaking, A.M. and P.M. refer to *solar* noon. Solar noon in any position on earth occurs when the sun crosses the meridian there; it is used as the standard reference time.

d There are 24 hours or 1,440 minutes in a day. Each day the earth rotates once on its axis. Therefore, the sun crosses meridians separated by 1° every 4 minutes (or moves 15° every hour). The sun rises in the east and sets in the west (which indicates that the earth spins on its axis). So meridians east of Greenwich experience noon earlier than Greenwich, and meridians west of Greenwich experience noon later than Greenwich. If the time where Vince lives is one hour ahead of Greenwich, then he must be 15 degrees east of Greenwich.

e i [Table 5.1–see page 229]
ii [Table 5.2–see page230]

f i In the tables **ei** and **eii**, note that as the 180° meridian is approached from the west, the TLT approaches 07:00 Tuesday. As the 180° meridian is approached from the east, the TLT approaches 07:00 Wednesday. However, 180°W = 180° E, so as the 180° meridian is crossed, the time must change by 24 hours. The 180° meridian is called the international date line.

ii 195° in the first table is 6:00 A.M. Wednesday because 24 hours has been gained by crossing the international date line, and longitude 195° is the same as longitude 165° traveling *east* of Greenwich. Similarly, longitude 195° on the second table is the same as longitude 165° traveling *west* of Greenwich (and 24 hours are lost by crossing the date line).

g The formula that relates west longitude *x* and true local time *t* is $TLT = GMT - \frac{x}{15}$. A 15° rotation of the earth takes one hour, so a 1° rotation takes 4 minutes. Therefore, if the local time is 17:48, it is 1 hour and 12 minutes behind 19:00 GMT, or 72 minutes behind. 72 ÷ 4 = 18, so the longitude is 18°W.

h For east longitude *y*, $TLT = GMT + \frac{y}{15}$.

i

TLT (hour)	Longitude
07:44	19°W
17:26	44°E
18:36	99°E
21:01	41°W
10:22	94°W

ii

GMT	TLT (hour)
12:00	12:24
14:00	11:36
13:30	17:22
20:00	12:00
04:00	12:00

2 **a i** 07:32 to 03:44—or 7:32 A.M. to 3:44 A.M. moving west.
ii 07:32 to 23:44—or 7:32 A.M. to 11:44 P.M. moving west. That's because the tip of the Aleutian Islands in Alaska is at longitude 176°E. (Note that the international date line is crossed at 180°W, so the end of the range of local times is 11:44 P.M. the *following day*.)
iii Yes—the eastern end of the Aleutian Islands in Alaska (approximately).
b Yes. However, since constantly changing time standards are very inconvenient, time zones have been established; watches need to be changed only at the boundaries of these time zones.

On Your Own   **Page 148**

Irregularities occur because the time zones are designed to keep countries that do not cover a wide band of longitudes within one time zone. Multiple time zones in large countries (such as the United States) usually have time-zone boundaries that follow state or provincial lines.

---

3 **a** True local time in Melbourne is 21:40 Friday. True local time in Rio de Janeiro is 09:08 Friday. The difference is 12 hours and 32 minutes.
b According to the map, Melbourne time is 9:30 P.M. (21:30) and Rio de Janeiro time is 9:00 A.M. (09:00). This is close to the true local times calculated but not exact.

c As it gets nearer the pole, it cuts across lines of longitude more frequently, which would mean rapid changes in time zones.

4 **a** Butter will melt (because of warm weather) somewhere off West Africa, which is about the same latitude as the West Indies. That means the advice is good.
b On the ship, the sun is at its highest 4 hours and 32 minutes before it is directly over Greenwich. This time difference of 272 minutes is equivalent to a longitude change of 68°. (Remember that there are 15° per hour of difference—and 1° per 4 minutes.) So the ship is 68°E of Greenwich.
c A minute lost per day for 28 days (4 weeks) is an extra 7° longitude that the ship has gained. So the ship's longitude is 68°E + 7°E = 75°E. In other words, when the navigator notes that the sun is highest at 07:28, it is really 07:00 in Greenwich.
d A ship's navigators could then read the GMT time on their clock at local solar noon and use the time difference to accurately calculate their longitude position.

5 **a** 12:00 is usually referred to as midday or noon, but it is midday by convention only. True midday, or *solar noon,* actually occurs midway between the times for sunrise and sunset, when the sun reaches its highest point in the sky.
b Solar noon occurs in the exact middle of the day—or halfway between the time of sunrise and sunset, which is 12:23.
c Jonathan is correct.
d 12:23

6 **a** June 15, September 1, and December 20 (approximately)
b The graph shows that solar noon at Greenwich occurs about 10 minutes before GMT noon.
c i 12:15
  ii 12:05
  iii 12:03
  iv 11:50
d i 12:15
  ii The time between 08:27 and 12:15 is 3 hours and 48 minutes.
  iii 3 hours and 48 minutes = 228 minutes. 228 ÷ 4 = 57°. Points east of Greenwich have their solar noon earlier than Greenwich, so the sailor is 57°E, not 57°W.
e [Table 5.5—see p. 230]
f i The shaded area above the axis is the same as the area below the axis.
  ii 12:00
  iii On the average (or mean), the sun is at its highest point over Greenwich at 12:00 Greenwich Mean Time.

---

1 Boston's center is at about 71°W, and Philadelphia's center is at about 75°W.

2 According to the graph, Greenwich solar noon is at 11:45 GMT. So on October 31, the solar noon for Boston is 16:29 GMT and for Philadelphia 16:45 GMT.

3 On October 31, the Eastern Standard Time of local solar noon in Boston is 11:29 A.M. and in Philadelphia 11:45 A.M. (You subtract 5 hours to account for the time difference.) Noon as shown on the clock occurs simultaneously, of course, in both cities at 12:00 P.M. because they are in the same time zone.

4 Chicago's center is at about 87°W. Dallas' center is at about 96°W. On October 31, the solar noon for Chicago is 17:33 GMT and for Dallas 18:09 GMT. The Central Standard Time of local solar noon in Chicago is 11:33 A.M. and in Dallas 12:09 P.M. Noon as shown on the clock occurs simultaneously, of course, in both cities at 12:00 P.M. because they are in the same time zone.

5 Answers will vary.

Investigation Four — Navigating by the Stars

1 **a** i Yes. Japan lies between latitudes 26°N and 46°N, which matches approximately his original latitude of 37°N.

b Yes. Columbus landed in the West Indies, not in Virginia. (Virginia is on latitude 37°N.)

2 **a** i Polaris remains fixed.
ii They will appear to move in a circle around Polaris; no other stars will appear stationary.
iii The point where a vertical line from Polaris touches the horizon will be due north of the ship. Knowing which way is north allows the navigator to steer the ship on a straight course. However, if there are clouds in the sky, the navigator can no longer be sure which direction is north.

b i About 40,000,000,000,000 kilometers
ii In theory, the light rays are not parallel, since they diverge in all directions as they leave the light source. However, even the sun is far enough away so that for all practical purposes its rays or those from any other star appear parallel and can be treated as such.

c i $\angle OPN = 90° - y$ and $\angle OPT = 90°$.

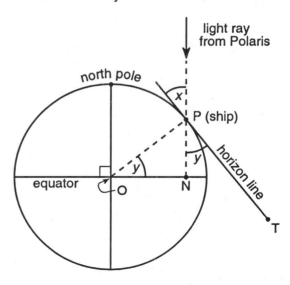

So $\angle NPT = y = x$, because x and $\angle NPT$ are vertical (opposite each other).
ii Polaris would be directly overhead, and your latitude would be 90°N. That's because an imaginary line drawn from the North Pole to the center of the earth and another line drawn from the equator create a 90° angle of latitude.

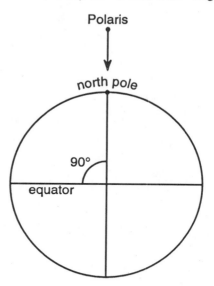

3 The sun is a star, and stars act in the same way as the sun. For example, the sun rises in the east and sets in the west. So do stars. In fact, the rising and setting of the sun and the stars is not caused by any movement of the star but by the rotation of the earth on its axis. The earth completes a full revolution every 24 hours. When a star is directly overhead, it is just crossing the meridian on which the observer is located. Following a star from its highest point (zenith) to where it falls to the horizon will locate the direction of west.

On Your Own — Page 155

1 Even quite small errors would be dangerous, as virtually all the islands in Polynesia are tiny and very easy to miss.

2 **a** Wind direction is typically east to west, so large ocean swells (waves) generally move in a westerly direction.
b The direction of the swells provides a more consistent westerly bearing than the wind, since storms can cause a change in wind direction while the big swells continue to move west for some time after a change in wind direction.
c Following the direction of birds (either from where they came or are headed) and going in the opposite direction often leads to landfall.
d Floating coconuts or other land plant matter are signs of an island nearby.

4 **b** The result of problem **2 c** shows that the ship must be on latitude 30°N (since the latitude equals the elevation of Polaris above the horizon). So the ship could be at San Antonio, Texas, New Orleans, Louisiana, Alexandria, Egypt, or any point in between.

5 **c** In this position, the string circle for 40° latitude represents a "latitude" relative to an axis through the center of the earth, the geographical position of the star, and the star itself. Hannah will be at some position on this 40°-"latitude" circle—just as she is on some position on the 60°N-latitude circle relative to Polaris and the north pole.
d The two latitude circles intersect in two points typically separated by hundreds of miles. Hannah will know which of the two is her location if she has kept track of her position from previous days. Only one of the two positions will make sense.

7 **a** A three-star fix will eliminate one of the two possible points in the two-star fix. The smaller the triangle, the more accurate the fix.
b in the middle

On Your Own — Page 159

1 It moves along a fixed latitude.
2 No, latitude stays the same.
3 Yes. The more accurate the time, the more accurate the star fix will be.
4 Factors that can cause significant problems in star navigation are quite small errors in angle measurement and observing stars near the horizon in which their positions are distorted by other light coming through the atmosphere.

CHAPTER FIVE — CHECK-UP

1 52°W

2 **a** Since the longitude of San Francisco and Portland is the same, the airplane should travel due north.

b Their latitudes differ by 7°, which is $\frac{7}{360}$ of the earth's circumference. Therefore, the distance between the cities is $\frac{7}{360} \times 25,000 \approx 486$ miles.

OVERSIZED TABLES AND FIGURES

Table 1.1

Network	Number of Odds	Number of Evens	Is There a Solution?
i	2	1	No
ii	0	3	Yes
iii	0	6	Yes
iv	2	2	No
v	4	2	No
vi	0	7	Yes
vii	0	6	Yes
viii	4	1	No
ix	0	8	Yes

Figure 1

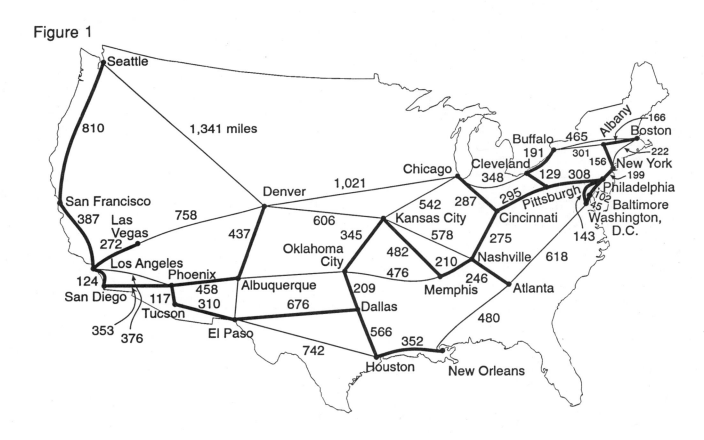

Table 2.3

v	A	B	C	D	E	F
A	x	1	2	3	4	5
B	1	x	3	4	5	2
C	2	3	x	5	1	4
D	3	4	5	x	2	1
E	4	5	1	2	x	3
F	5	2	4	1	3	x

Table 2.4

Round 1	Round 2	Round 3	Round 4	Round 5
A v B	A v C	A v D	A v E	A v F
C v E	B v F	B v C	B v D	B v E
D v F	D v E	E v F	C v F	C v D

Table 2.5

v	A	B	C	D	E	F	G	H
A	x	1	2	3	4	5	6	7
B	1	x	3	4	5	6	7	2
C	2	3	x	5	6	7	1	4
D	3	4	5	x	7	1	2	6
E	4	5	6	7	x	2	3	1
F	5	6	7	1	2	x	4	3
G	6	7	1	2	3	4	x	5
H	7	2	4	6	1	3	5	x

Table 2.6

v	A	B	C	D	E	F	G	H	I	J
A	x	1	2	3	4	5	6	7	8	9
B	1	x	3	4	5	6	7	8	9	2
C	2	3	x	5	6	7	8	9	1	4
D	3	4	5	x	7	8	9	1	2	6
E	4	5	6	7	x	9	1	2	3	8
F	5	6	7	8	9	x	2	3	4	1
G	6	7	8	9	1	2	x	4	5	3
H	7	8	9	1	2	3	4	x	6	5
I	8	9	1	2	3	4	5	6	x	7
J	9	2	4	6	8	1	3	5	7	x

Table 2.14

3-pointers	2-pointers	1-pointers	Total
4	2	8	24
2	5	8	24
0	8	8	24

Table 2.15

	1	2	3	5	10	20	25	50	Total Points
Pedro	1	1	1	0	0	2	1	0	71
Kyla	1	1	1	1	1	0	0	1	71
Maureen	1	0	0	1	2	1	1	0	71
Totals	3	2	2	2	3	3	2	1	213

Table 2.18

Speed (m/s)		Time (s)		Total Time (s)	Average Speed of Rabbit (m/s to nearest tenth)
Lap 1	Lap 2	Lap 1	Lap 2		
20	10	20	40	60	13.3
5	20	80	20	100	8
8	10	50	40	90	8.9
10	2	40	200	240	3.3
1	20	400	20	420	1.9

Table 2.19

Round 1	Round 2	Round 3	Round 4	Round 5
A ∨ O	O ∨ C	O ∨ N	O ∨ W	C ∨ N
C ∨ W	N ∨ W	A ∨ C	A ∨ N	W ∨ A

Table 2.20

Touchdowns

		0	1	2	3	4	5
	0	0	7	14	21	28	35
	1	4	11	18	25	32	39
	2	8	15	22	29	36	43
Field	3	12	19	26	33	40	47
Goals	4	16	23	30	37	44	51
	5	20	27	34	41	48	55
	6	24	31	38	45	52	59
	7	28	35	42	49	56	63
	8	32	39	46	53	60	67
	9	36	43	50	57	64	71

Table 2.21

Name	Goals scored	Games played	Goals/game
Margaret	**100**	5	20
Rhonda	84	4	**21**
Susan	**56**	2	28
Kay	120	**5**	24
Totals	360	16	**22.5**

Table 3.1

Formula	Name	Related Alcohol
HCHO	methanal or formaldehyde	methanol (methyl alcohol)
CH_3CHO	ethanal or acetaldehyde	ethanol (ethyl alcohol)
C_2H_5CHO	propanal or propionaldehyde	propanol (propyl alcohol)

Table 3.2

Structure	Common Name	Where It Is Found
$CH_3(CH_2)_{16}COOH$	stearic acid	mainly in animal fats
$CH_3(CH_2)_{10}COOH$	lauric acid	coconut and palm-kernel oil
$CH_3(CH_2)_{14}COOH$	palmitic acid	most fats, especially palm oil
$CH_3(CH_2)_7CH =$ $CH(CH_2)_7COOH$	oleic acid	most fats, especially olive oil

Table 3.17

x	y	First Difference	Second Difference
0	c		
		$a + b$	
1	$a + b + c$		$2a$
		$3a + b$	
2	$4a + 2b + c$		$2a$
		$5a + b$	
3	$9a + 3b + c$		$2a$
		$7a + b$	
4	$16a + 4b + c$		

Table 3.26

Number of Frogs of Each Color	Number of Hops	Number of Jumps
1	2	1
2	4	4
3	6	9
4	8	16
n	$2n$	n^2

Table 3.27

x	y	First Difference	Second Difference	Third Difference
0	0			
		1		
1	1		3	
		4		2
2	5		5	
		9		2
3	14		7	
		16		2
4	30		9	
		25		
5	55			

Table 3.28

x	y	First Difference	Second Difference	Third Difference
0	d			
		$a+b+c$		
1	$a+b+c+d$		$6a+2b$	
		$7a+3b+c$		$6a$
2	$8a+4b+2c+d$		$12a+2b$	
		$19a+5b+c$		$6a$
3	$27a+9b+3c+d$		$18a+2b$	
		$37a+7b+c$		$6a$
4	$64a+16b+4c+d$		$24a+2b$	
		$61a+9b+c$		
5	$125a+25b+5c+d$			

Table 3.29

	1×1	1×2	1×3	1×4	2×2	2×3	2×4	3×3	3×4	4×4	Total
A (1×1)	1	-	-	-	-	-	-	-	-	-	$1 = 1^2$
B (2×2)	4	4	-	-	1	-	-	-	-	-	$9 = 3^2$
C (3×3)	9	12	6	-	4	4	-	1	-	-	$36 = 6^2$
D (4×4)	16	24	16	8	9	12	6	4	4	1	$100 = 10^2$

Table 3.30

Side of Square	Number of Rectangles
1	1^2
2	$3^2 = (1 + 2)^2$
3	$6^2 = (1 + 2 + 3)^2$
4	$10^2 = (1 + 2 + 3 + 4)^2$
n	$(1 + 2 + 3 + 4 + \ldots + n)^2$

Table 4.2

t (h)	p (g)	Pattern
0	0	0.5 × 0
2	1	0.5 × 2
4	2	0.5 × 4
6	3	0.5 × 6
8	4	0.5 × 8
t	p	0.5 × t

$p=0.5t$

Table 4.3

Engine	t (h)	p (g)	Formula
1	6	3	$p = 0.5t$
2	8	6	$p = 0.75t$
3	10	7	$p = 0.7t$
4	20	19	$p = 0.95t$
5	100	63	$p = 0.63t$
6	3	6	$p = 2t$
7	4	2.4	$p = 0.6t$
8	10	18	$p = 1.8t$
9	5	9	$p = 1.8t$
10	5	20	$p = 4t$

Table 4.5

Firm	Equation	Cost of Calculator ($)	Postage ($)
M.Y. Martin	$C = 21.49x + 3.00$	21.49	3.00
Cheapsales, Inc.	$C = 19.99x + 7.30$	19.99	7.30
Brown & Brown	$C = 20.25x + 3.80$	20.25	3.80
Ron Ripper, Inc.	$C = 24.49x + 6.30$	24.49	6.30
Discounters, Inc.	$C = 21.00x + 3.50$	21.00	3.50

Table 4.6

Name	Equation	Speed (m/s)	Handicap (m)
Marilyn	$d = 8t + 12$	8	12.0
Lesley	$d = 7.5t + 15.2$	7.5	15.2
Anna	$d = 8.6t + 5.2$	8.6	5.2
Hannah	$d = 7.3t + 14$	7.3	14
Ruth	$d = 8.1t + 5.6$	8.1	5.6
Crystal	$d = 9.0t$	9.0	0

Table 4.7

Runner	Constant Speed (ft/s) (1)	Time for 1 foot (s) (2)	Time for 1 mile (s)	Time for 1 mile (min and s)
Rosa	15	0.0666666	351.999648	5:52
Leanne	14	0.0714286	377.143008	6:17
Randy	11	0.0909091	480.000048	8:00
Murray	12	0.0833333	439.999824	7:20
Peter	10	0.1000000	528	8:48
Kevin	16	0.0625000	330	5:30

Table 4.12

Time Interval (seconds)	Distance Traveled (meters)	Average Speed (m/s)
0.0–0.5	8.75 − 0.0 = 8.75	17.5
0.5–1.0	15 − 8.75 = 6.25	12.5
1.0–1.5	18.75 − 15 = 3.75	7.5
1.5–2.0	20 − 18.75 = 1.25	2.5
2.0–2.5	18.75 − 20 = ⁻1.25	−2.5
2.5–3.0	15 − 18.75 = ⁻3.75	−7.5
3.0–3.5	8.75 − 15.00 = ⁻6.25	−12.5
3.5–4.0	0 − 8.75 = ⁻8.75	−17.5

Table 4.15

Time at Start t_1 (seconds)	Distance from Start d_1 (meters)	Time at End t_2 (seconds)	Distance from Start (d_2) (meters)	Average Speed in the Interval (meters/second)
2	4	5	25	$\dfrac{25 - 4}{5 - 2} = 7$
2	4	3	9	$\dfrac{9 - 4}{3 - 2} = 5$
3	9	4	16	$\dfrac{16 - 9}{4 - 3} = 7$
4	16	5	25	$\dfrac{25 - 16}{5 - 4} = 9$
0	0	3	9	$\dfrac{9 - 0}{3 - 0} = 3$
t_1	d_1	t_2	d_2	$\dfrac{d_2 - d_1}{t_2 - t_1}$

Table 4.16

Time at Start t_1 (seconds)	Water Escaped by Start w_1 (m^3)	Time at End t_2 (seconds)	Water escaped by End w_2 (m^3)	Average Rate of Water Loss (m^3/second)
0	0	1	5	$\dfrac{5 - 0}{1 - 0} = 5$
1	5	2	20	$\dfrac{20 - 5}{2 - 1} = 15$
2	20	3	45	$\dfrac{45 - 20}{3 - 2} = 25$
3	45	4	80	$\dfrac{80 - 45}{4 - 3} = 35$
4	80	5	125	$\dfrac{125 - 80}{5 - 4} = 45$
2	20	5	125	$\dfrac{125 - 20}{5 - 2} = 35$
0	0	5	125	$\dfrac{125 - 0}{5 - 0} = 25$
t_1	w_1	t_2	w_2	$\dfrac{w_2 - w_1}{t_2 - t_1}$

Table 4.17

Time Just Before Radar Gun Seen t (seconds)	Distance at Time t (feet)	Time on Seeing Radar Gun (seconds)	Distance When Radar Gun Seen (feet)	Average Speed (feet/second)
2.9	6×2.9^2	3	6×3^2	$\dfrac{6 \times 3^2 - 6 \times 2.9^2}{3 - 2.9} = 35.4$
2.9	6×2.99^2	3	6×3^2	$\dfrac{6 \times 3^2 - 6 \times 2.99^2}{0.01} = 35.94$
2.999	6×2.999^2	3	6×3^2	$\dfrac{6 \times 3^2 - 6 \times 2.999^2}{0.001} = 35.994$

Table 4.19

Time Just Before Impact t (seconds)	Distance at Time t (meters)	Time to Impact (seconds)	Distance to Impact (meters)	Average Speed (meters/second)
2.9	5×2.9^2	3	45	29.5
2.99	5×2.99^2	3	45	29.95
2.999	5×2.999^2	3	45	29.995

Table 4.23

Time just Before Collision t (seconds)	Distance Traveled t (meters)	Time to Collision (seconds)	Distance to Collision (meters)	Average Speed (meters/second)
3.9	20.305	4	21	6.95
3.99	20.930	4	21	6.995
3.999	20.993	4	21	6.9995

Table 4.27

x (length)	y (width)	Pattern in y
0	20	$20 - 0$
1	19	$20 - 1$
2	18	$20 - 2$
3	17	$20 - 3$
4	16	$20 - 4$
x	y	$20 - x$

Table 4.28

x (length)	y (width)	Pattern in y
0	200	200 − (2 × 0)
10	180	200 − (2 × 10)
20	160	**200 − (2 × 20)**
30	**140**	**200 − (2 × 30)**
40	**120**	**200 − (2 × 40)**
x	y	200 − (2 × **x**)

Figure 2

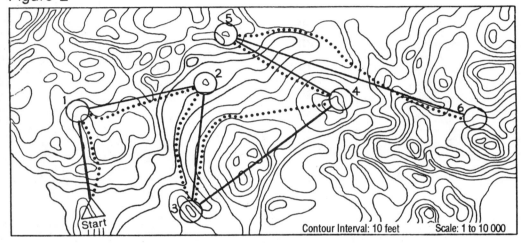

Contour Interval: 10 feet   Scale: 1 to 10 000

Table 5.1

West of Greenwich

Longitude(x)	True Local Time (t)	Clock Time
0°	19:00 Tuesday (GMT)	7:00 P.M.
15°	18:00 Tuesday	6:00 P.M.
30°	**17:00 Tuesday**	**5:00 P.M.**
45°	**16:00 Tuesday**	**4:00 P.M.**
60°	**15:00 Tuesday**	**3:00 P.M.**
75°	**14:00 Tuesday**	**2:00 P.M.**
90°	**13:00 Tuesday**	**1:00 P.M.**
105°	**12:00 Tuesday**	**12:00 (noon)**
120°	**11:00 Tuesday**	11:00 A.M.
135°	**10:00 Tuesday**	10:00 A.M.
150°	**09:00 Tuesday**	9:00 A.M.
165°	**08:00 Tuesday**	8:00 A.M.
180°	**07:00 Tuesday**	7:00 A.M.
195°	**06:00 Wednesday**	6:00 A.M.

Table 5.2

East of Greenwich

Longitude(y)	True Local Time (t)	Clock Time
0°	19:00 Tuesday (GMT)	7:00 P.M.
15°	20:00 Tuesday	8:00 P.M.
30°	21:00 Tuesday	9:00 P.M.
45°	22:00 Tuesday	10:00 P.M.
60°	23:00 Tuesday	11:00 P.M.
75°	00:00 (midnight)	12:00 A.M.
90°	01:00 Wednesday	1:00 A.M.
105°	02:00 Wednesday	2:00 A.M.
120°	03:00 Wednesday	3:00 A.M.
135°	04:00 Wednesday	4:00 A.M.
150°	05:00 Wednesday	5:00 A.M.
165°	06:00 Wednesday	6:00 A.M.
180°	07:00 Wednesday	7:00 A.M.
195°	08:00 Tuesday	8:00 A.M.

Table 5.5

Date at Greenwich	Local Solar Noon (GMT)	Greenwich Solar Noon GMT) on this Date	Difference	Longitude (Nearest Degree)
Feb 12	08:27	12:15	3 hours, 48 minutes	57°E
April 15	08:00	12:00	4 hours	60°E
July 31	21:07	12:08	8 hours, 59 minutes	135°W
Sept 1	03:05	12:00	8 hours, 55 minutes	134°E
Oct 31	00:02	11:46	11 hours, 44 minutes	176°E
May 15	22:41	11:58	10 hours, 43 minutes	161°W
March 15	12:04	12:08	4 minutes	1°E
Jan 31	00:47	12:14	11 hours, 27 minutes	172°E